Dear Dr. Rodger,

Thank you for your insightful contributions to leadership & innovation. I hope you find value in the perspectives shared in this book.

Wishing you continued success & inspiring leadership!

Best,

FAILING FAST?

LUV TULSIDAS

FAILING FAST?

THE (10) SECRETS TO SUCCEED FASTER

{ innovation done right }

Forbes | Books

Published by Forbes Books, Charleston, South Carolina.
An imprint of Advantage Media Group.

Forbes Books is a registered trademark, and the Forbes Books colophon is a trademark of Forbes Media, LLC.

Printed in the United States of America.

10 9 8 7 6 5 4 3 2 1

ISBN: 978-1-955884-90-7 (Hardcover)
ISBN: 978-1-955884-91-4 (eBook)

Library of Congress Control Number: 2023923222

Cover design by Pradnya Mahajan.

This custom publication is intended to provide accurate information and the opinions of the author in regard to the subject matter covered. It is sold with the understanding that the publisher, Forbes Books, is not engaged in rendering legal, financial, or professional services of any kind. If legal advice or other expert assistance is required, the reader is advised to seek the services of a competent professional.

Since 1917, Forbes has remained steadfast in its mission to serve as the defining voice of entrepreneurial capitalism. Forbes Books, launched in 2016 through a partnership with Advantage Media, furthers that aim by helping business and thought leaders bring their stories, passion, and knowledge to the forefront in custom books. Opinions expressed by Forbes Books authors are their own. To be considered for publication, please visit **books.Forbes.com**.

CONTENTS

Part II: The Succeed-Faster Method

Part III: The Succeed-Faster Execution

INTRODUCTION

While the world demands more meaningful innovation from business leaders, the current paradigm for delivering that innovation is not working anymore! The prevailing workplace culture has inadvertently slowed the pace of much-needed transformations.

What do you expect to happen when the popular culture in business embraces the principle of fail fast, fail often, and pivot often? More success? More breakthroughs?

As a wise person said a long time ago, "Life will give you more of what you wish for." Therefore, I say to the wise people of today, "Be more mindful of what you wish for!"

Enterprises cannot afford to fail at producing useful innovations because unprecedented disruptions are now imminent as a result of the recent advancements in Artificial Intelligence (AI). This evolution coincides with a seismic socioeconomic shift that is in progress across the world. Companies that want to be taken seriously must have the following co-existing agendas in their vision: (1) Generate bigger profits and (2) Deliver significantly more value for the communities they serve. The only way to achieve this is by succeeding faster and more cost-effectively at innovation. In other words, "Innovation Done Right!"

The ten secrets to succeeding faster in this book have been a career saver for established CEOs and enterprise leaders. Particularly, when they had no choice but to transform their companies by delivering innovations their businesses needed to stay relevant. These secrets also helped many entrepreneurs succeed with the limited funding and the short runway that startups get to execute their vision. In these volatile times, we need leaders and dreamers like you to be empowered with a new mindset and a highly effective method to build your dreams of the future without having to rely on luck. Ironically, people like to rely on luck even though luck is unreliable by nature. Without further ado, let me introduce you to the most powerful concepts that you will learn in this book:

- Succeed faster by aligning with the extremely powerful market forces—the zeitgeist!

- Work smarter before working harder to succeed faster in these disruptive times.

- Build a strong vision to lead you through the distractions on the way to your destination.

- Build an invincible team that will burn on through the impossible times.

- Most important, find your winning wow factor, and choose the right day 1 customer before wasting your resources on building your vision of the future!

Who Is This Book For?

Whether you are a CEO looking to modernize your established enterprise or you are a board member trusted by shareholders to influence a more exciting future for your business.

Whether you are a visionary entrepreneur building a company to change the world or you are an intrapreneur developing a game-changing solution for the organization where you work.

Whether you are an ambitious student or you are a "nobody" who aspires to build their grand vision of the future.

Regardless of where you are in your life journey, you will find the secrets in this book highly valuable if you have the need to deliver meaningful innovation for your market fast enough to get ahead of the rest.

Wouldn't it be nice if our dreams could manifest themselves by waving our magic wands? OK, I know that's a little too much of a fairy-tale talk for a book of this genre. But for too long now, the business world has been following a fairy-tale approach to innovation: fail fast, fail often, and pivot often. Try again and again, fail over and over, until you achieve success.

The evidence that this popular methodology has not been effective is in the fact that 80 percent of transformation initiatives and innovation projects in enterprises fail to deliver their intended value. I have personally witnessed this as an employee of a major company and, more recently, as the leader of a consulting firm helping many legacy enterprises transform themselves to avoid the fate of these statistics.

Startups are supposed to be nimble and more efficient. Conventional wisdom says that startups must be doing much better because they don't have all the legacy baggage and the infamous technical debt of older businesses. Is that true? Consider the shocking fact that 90 percent of startups go out of business before achieving their vision within the first five years.

This strategy is not meant for 99.9 percent of us because most people and businesses cannot afford to take major risks again after failing at their first moonshot. Nonetheless, this has somehow become the mainstream business approach to innovation.

So, who is responsible for all the waste and inefficiencies that exist in business today?

The "catch me if you can" business leader! It is undeniable that the people responsible to lead us, CEOs and executive leaders, are failing in high numbers.

Modern CEOs and business leaders have become very good at playing "catch me if you can," as depicted in the famous movie by the same title. According to recent surveys, the median tenure of a CEO in a company is down to a record low of five years, and executive leaders have an even lower life span on the job.[1] The world is changing so drastically that no company vision can be taken seriously today without innovation being at its core.

Innovation is hard. Wait, that is wrong, so let me correct myself. Innovation is very very hard! It takes about five years to deliver on a good vision, and the data shows us that most company leaders are not able to deliver on their vision. So they are getting fired or conveniently leaving for the next job when their five-year vision comes due. They say "catch me if you can" to their outgoing company, while they move on to a new job to repeat the same cycle every three to five years.

What should we do? Keep on firing and replacing the executives every five years? Maybe we should fire them faster. Every two years would be better?

---

1   PwC, "CEO turnover at record high; successors following long serving CEOs struggling according to PwC's Strategy & Global Study," PwC, accessed November 20, 2023, https://www.pwc.com/gx/en/news-room/press-releases/2019/ceo-turnover-record-high.html#.

When a problem is this systemic, firing people is not going to get us anywhere. This is not a people problem. The root cause lies in the mindset and methods being used for innovation by companies today. They are clearly not working anymore!

The seasoned leaders are well aware of this risk, so they tend to avoid taking on major innovations for their business. While that appears to be a safer approach, especially for those closer to retirement, it is becoming less viable of an option for executive leaders. This is because the world is approaching the point of inflection with rapidly evolving geopolitical, macroeconomic, and technological shifts converging at once.

So, something significant has to change, and that change has to happen fast.

Why Should You Listen to Me?

I would love to tell you that I was born a prodigy, and one day I woke up with an epiphany of the ten secrets to conquer business innovation.

But the truth is that in the first four decades of my life, I worked very hard to acquire the knowledge and skills that I didn't have but needed to keep up with my ambitions. The silver lining is that because I earned my path to success the hard way, I am now able to articulate for you, through this book, the important lessons I have learned on my journey from there to here.

I was born with subpar physical traits, intelligence, and personality. My formative years were filled with challenges, and I had no achievements to show for during this period. However, I was blessed with the natural ability to dream about big and unrealistic things that I had no idea how to accomplish. There is a long list of celebrity entrepreneurs who did not make it through college. I did better than them. I did not graduate high school! This may be a shock to many who know me as I am revealing this personal secret for the first time.

Wait, but there is a twist to this story. Somehow, I hustled my way from my birthplace on a tiny island in Africa to a reputable engineering university across the world in the United States, without a high school degree. How that happened is a story for another time.

In college, I barely managed to survive academically and took much longer than most in my cohort to graduate. Society had written me off because I didn't look or sound like someone who had a chance to become successful. I could not articulate my superpower to anyone without being laughed off. Yet, deep in my heart, I knew that someday, somehow, I would build something very special that would bring a lot of value to the world, and in the process, I would become very successful.

I did not know exactly how I would get there for the first two decades of my life, but I was not willing to accept the fate that others had decided for me. So, I worked very hard after college to acquire the necessary skills and found a way to rapidly catch up with my larger-than-life ambitions. Often, I sacrificed personal relationships to overcome my gaps. Once, I worked forty-eight hours straight to accomplish a mission impossible at my first corporate job. This phase of my life taught me what actually works and what doesn't.

The most valuable lessons I learned came across the spectrum of a fifteen-year career as an employee and a leader at a large enterprise, followed by the last seven years as a founder, entrepreneur, and CEO of my startup—Techolution.

I started my career in the corporate world as an entry-level employee. My superpower as a dreamer combined with a solid work ethic led me to become an intrapreneur. I built the digital platform for one of the oldest and most recognized brands in the world from zero to $5 billion per year in less than six years. Over the past seven years, I had an amazing journey as a founder of the company that I started with nothing but a dream and the gracious support of my wife.

Today, with the partnership of some amazing leaders and a great team, I have built Techolution to be an admirable brand that transforms traditional enterprises with "Innovation done right." We are a consulting firm that helps our clients innovate their business at a guaranteed price by leveraging the power of novel technologies, such as real-world AI, to help them thrive in this new era.

In 2019, I won the prestigious Inc. 500 award on behalf of Techolution, for being one of the fastest-growing companies in America. In 2022, Techolution proudly received the Best-in-Business award for being the best in our industry. While building Techolution to become the brand that is admired for "Innovation done right" across the world, I had the privilege of working with a variety of businesses on their major transformation initiatives. As we were earning a reputation for delivering hyper-velocity success on impossible innovation projects for major clients, my business was growing rapidly. On the personal side, my family was also growing, and I was accumulating more gray hair by the day. When I could not possibly work harder anymore, I had no choice but to become obsessed with finding a smarter way to succeed faster and further.

After years of research and real-world testing, I have meticulously curated the top ten most effective secrets to help you avoid the common mistakes most people make on their journey to build their innovative ideas. It is time to stop failing fast and start succeeding faster and winning more often.

Ultimately, my motivation for taking on the monumental effort of writing a book about a complex topic like this while still leading a growing company full-time is very personal. I want to help as many people who have the desire to build successful businesses to make sure they do it faster, and in a way, that will lead to a better world for our kids. The world needs more people like us to win faster. So, let's channel our dreams and magnify our superpowers to leave a legacy that will be appreciated for generations to come.

INTRODUCTION – KEY TAKEAWAYS

YOUR NOTES

_____

_____

_____

_____

_____

_____

_____

_____

_____

_____

_____

_____

_____

PART I

THE SUCCEED-FASTER MINDSET

*Learn the **mindset** required to help you succeed faster and win consistently.*

Succeed Faster **SECRET #1**

Dream Big and Do Bold

*are the two ingredients you need
to get started on the journey to
succeeding faster at your big goals.*

CHAPTER 1

DREAM BIG AND DO BOLD

O ur world is at a critical inflection point. Technology has unquestionably become an integral part of our lives. At the current pace of innovation, the way we experience life on this planet will drastically change by the end of this decade and beyond. The good news is how the current spurt of evolution ends up impacting our lives remains undecided. And the bad news is there isn't much time left to roll up our sleeves and influence the final outcome.

While the universe has been continuously changing since the beginning of time, meaningful evolution happens in waves. Right now, we are in the early stages of a new zeitgeist. How these incoming new waves of innovation will impact our civilization is yet to be determined. What we know for sure is that there are two distinct possibilities.

The first option is pretty dire. In this scenario, we end up with a world that has humans addicted and enslaved by their own innovative creations, benefiting a few forces in the world who are abusing the rest of us for their greed and power. They are making strides toward deploying new technologies to make this grim version a reality.

The alternate possibility is a much more positive one, where we innovate with the primary purpose of enriching the human experience. The leaders who do the hard work and take the risks to make the change happen will be well rewarded. In this version, we won't have to choose between doing good for society versus economic growth. We won't need to worry about working stressful mundane jobs versus losing our livelihoods to automation. As a result of our own creations working for us, we will have an abundance of opportunities so that everyone can live to their fullest potential without discrimination.

It is still possible to build a world where innovation, corporate profits, and meaningful social causes come together to create an unstoppable force for good. In this book, we will explore such a win-win model that is urgently needed to prevent a major revolution currently developing because of the growing divide between the rich and the poor, the left and the right, the super successful and the 99 percent of the population.

So, are you going to sit on the sideline and just watch how it goes? Or,

Are you going to be a force for good and make your impact on what happens next?

Whether you were born average or talented, whether you are privileged or underprivileged, it doesn't really matter because,

Only those who dare to dream big and have the courage to do bold stand a chance to achieve great things in life.

But wait, is dreaming big going to be enough to succeed?

While our ability to dream big and our warrior-like courage to make bold moves are the fuel that is needed to get through the treacherous journey of dream building, it is not going to be enough.

Even the most ambitious of the visionaries and bravest of the brave end up "dying a slow death by one thousand cuts" on their journey to success.

I have always been a dreamer. Ever since I was young, I struggled to wake up in the morning because I couldn't sleep at night. As a child, I grew up in a very normal, happy, and stable home. I had a role model father, a loving mother, a bright older sister, and an adorable younger brother. We were not wealthy, but we lived well, and all our basic needs were fulfilled.

Every night, when my father returned from work, we would all sit at the dinner table as a family, say a prayer, and eat the delicious dinner that my mother cooked. After dinner, we would finish homework and watch TV together as a family. By 10:00 p.m., everyone went to their bedrooms, and the lights were off.

When it was quiet outside and the whole world was falling asleep, my vivid imagination would come alive. While lying in bed and staring at the ceiling in pitch dark, my mind would go on these wild adventures. I could not help but get lost in the thoughts of something big that I would invent and build in the future.

My open-eyed dreams were often larger than life and way beyond my league at the time. At 2:00 a.m., my adrenaline would be pumping at full speed, and I would not be tired enough to fall asleep until after 4 a.m. Often, I would see the crack of dawn before my eyes would close for the night. As a result, I would get in trouble the next day. School started at 8:00 a.m. sharp, and every weekday morning, my father would wait in his car at 7:30 a.m. to drop all three of his kids to school. By 7:40 a.m., my father would leave the house with only two of his three kids. The first few days of every school season, he would give me the benefit of the doubt and wait a little longer. But it wasn't fair to my sister and brother because waiting for me meant that they would all be late for their school.

As a result, I had to walk to school, which made me even more late and got me in even bigger trouble. My first-period teacher was very upset with me. The school had a very strict culture of discipline and punctuality. On top of that, my teacher was a man with a big ego. He felt that I was disrespecting him by coming late to his class in the morning. As a result, the teacher had to punish me in order to teach me a lesson about punctuality.

In today's world, these punishments would be considered physical abuse and illegal. Back in the 1980s, on the paradise island of Mauritius in Africa, in a post-British-colony democracy, it was not uncommon for teachers and other grown-ups to physically punish "bad" kids.

I was a very young boy, six years old to be precise, when my teacher asked me to stand on a classroom desk in front of my classmates as a punishment for being late to class. To be fair, he had given me verbal warnings on the first two days of school when I showed up late. For a shy kid like me, having to stand on a desk in front of my classmates was torturous enough, but this was the culture of the old colonial British education system that was pervasive in Mauritius at the time. Since this would not qualify as a real punishment, my teacher had to step it up a notch.

As I stood on my little classroom desk, some of my classmates burst into laughter. The teacher went on to ask the rest of the class to laugh at me. Those who were not laughing already obeyed and laughed out loud. Then the teacher went on to pull my pants down. As tears dropped from my eyes, with my naked butt exposed to the classroom mocking me, I froze! I was not able to say what I was thinking, "Sorry, I won't be late again, please stop." The teacher hit me hard with a thick wooden stick on my little six-year-old rear.

As the beating started, the entire first-grade classroom got quiet and watched in shock. The teacher asked, "Are you sorry? Will you ever be late again?" My throat choked so tight from a combination of fear and embarrassment that words would not come out of my mouth. Since the teacher did not hear me say "sorry" out loud, the beating continued for a few more minutes until he realized that if he didn't stop now, the visible damage might get to a level where he would bring a lot of negative attention from the authorities onto himself.

One would imagine that this kind of traumatic punishment would teach me a lesson about punctuality and I would never be late again. Quite the contrary happened. I was late to school again and again in spite of the brutal punishments that I dreaded. What nobody understood is that I was not intentionally going late to school to be rebellious. Becoming a "rebel without a cause" was the last thing on my mind. I had no intention to disrespect anyone. The problem was not in my control. I tried very hard to sleep on time at night, but I was not able to. I was not staying up late at night and waking up late in the morning on purpose. Since I was not a good communicator, nobody was interested in hearing my "excuses" about the adventurous open-eyed dreams that kept me up at night.

Eventually, my teacher gave up on trying to teach me punctuality. He asked me to wait outside of his classroom for the whole first period whenever I was late. That sounded like a more reasonable punishment for my inability to follow the rules. So, every morning, I stood outside of the classroom during the first period until the principal of the school took notice. The matter escalated into a bigger and more formal action that involved my parents!

Dreaming big was one of the only secrets to success that I did not have to learn the hard way in this life. I was born with it, and it stuck with me through good and bad times. I strongly believe that it's the only reason why I was able to defy all odds. It also allowed me to learn the other nine secrets of success that got me through my journey from there to here.

Success Is Uniquely Individual

I didn't write this book to motivate you to dream big. There are plenty of books and motivational speakers who have been doing that longer and better than I can. I assume that you already have a desire to accomplish something big and innovative. Why else would you read a book about succeeding faster at innovation?

My goal is to show you a battle-tested method to build your innovative idea effectively enough so that you can attain the "escape velocity" needed to get to your destination before running out of resources and ending up in the overcrowded graveyard of great ideas.

Learning from others can be helpful, but I have learned that ultimately, the best way to live your life is to:

Aspire to be the best version of yourself, or you will end up becoming a crappy version of someone else.

That is because,

Success is very individual in nature, and it is very difficult to equationize.

Therefore, I cannot tell you exactly what you need to build in order to be successful because the possibilities are endless. There are an infinite number of paths to success, and we all have our own unique perspectives and journeys that deserve to be respected. That is why you must pursue the dreams that you are passionate about and not try to achieve someone else's dream.

While I cannot tell you what dreams you must pursue, in this book, I will provide you with a framework to help you succeed faster by enabling you to rapidly discover a unique path that inspires you. This method comes paired with the guardrails necessary to prevent you from falling off your individually chosen track based on the common mistakes that people make on similar journeys.

Is the Popular Approach Working?

The popular leadership methods that we are taught in schools and the business world today do not work for 99.9 percent of us. The proof is that there are many more courageous people who have genuinely attempted to build their dream, but yet, they ended up failing fast and hard. Over 80 percent of innovation projects in enterprises fail to complete or deliver their intended value.[2] Case in point, the average tenure of a CEO is down to five years, and the executive leaders have an even lower life span on the job. Startups are supposed to be more efficient, but 90 percent of startups go out of business before achieving their vision.[3]

The media likes to glorify the "one-in-a-thousand" business leaders who made it big with their innovative ideas at a young age because it makes for a great entertaining hero story. What they don't show us is that for each "hero" success story, there are 999 others who have tried similar moves but failed. Most get burnt out of the game after their first failure and have no ability to try again, causing them to become risk-averse and robotic.

---

2   Board of Innovation, "Why your innovation experiments fail," accessed November 20, 2023, https://www.boardofinnovation.com/blog/why-your-innovation-experiments-fail/.

3   Startup Genome, "The State of the Global Economy," accessed November 20, 2023, https://startupgenome.com/article/the-state-of-the-global-startup-economy.

Failure is the natural state of things. You have to do nothing to fail.

Failure is a part of the common and boring life. Who wants to watch or read about all the failure stories? Hence, we do not get to hear about those who have failed in the media that we consume. This implicitly imprints in the minds of the public that we should be emulating the one-in-a-thousand business superstar who made it big if we want to become successful.

What I learnt from studying failure: The real reason for such a high rate of failure in the world is that the methods that we follow to execute our ideas were developed by the privileged 0.1 percent who were born with a special talent. They are teaching us the unique skills that they were gifted with as a "one-size-fits-all" success formula.

Who do you think benefits when the status quo system tells us to work harder for our entire adult life, until someday we are promised a chance to feel successful, before we drop dead, when we are old and ready to retire?

The mainstream principle of success "just keep on working harder" is not scalable. It took me too long to learn from my own experiences that working too hard for the sake of working hard makes us feel burnt out and clouds our judgment. As a result, we tend to become robotic and lead our way through the nuances of life as we have been programmed, whether it fits the situation or not.

As Albert Einstein famously said, "The definition of insanity is trying to do the same thing over and over again and expecting different results." Therefore, we have to question the popular principles and habits for success that we have been taught at school and in the workforce. We will need to unlearn these principles first and then substitute them with a more effective method that will help the 99.9 percent of us succeed faster.

Unlearn the Fail-Fast and Fail-Often Mindset

The fail-fast mindset is everywhere in our society today. Fail fast, fail often, and pivot often has been a very popular mantra in the business world since the last great financial crisis in 2008. Its primary purpose was to minimize the psychological and economic impact of losing. Keep on trying to fail rapidly and keep on pivoting until failure does not happen anymore. Hopefully, we will have gained enough momentum before running out of resources and energy from all the failures. How is a mindset that looks forward to failing fast and failing often still the de facto success formula in the world today?

Maybe for someone who is privileged with plenty of financial resources, it might be a fun adventure to take bold actions with the intention to fail. Most of us cannot afford to fail once, let alone failing often. In the event that we take a chance and fail, we will not have the luxury and the financial capability to pivot and start again and again until we find success.

As many of my friends in top leadership roles in some of the biggest companies in the world often say, "Let alone failing fast, failure just wasn't an option when I was faced with this crisis." In spite of this, the premier management consultants on their advisory board keep insisting that the only way to innovate and succeed in this new world is to celebrate failure and make failing fast a desirable goal.

When your reputation as a leader and the livelihoods of the people who depend on you are at stake, failure cannot be the outcome we should be looking forward to, regardless of how fast and often it is. For those of us who grew up failing often without intending to fail, we know that it isn't so cool to fail fast and fail often intentionally now that we have tasted some success and stability.

So, why are so many smart people in the world today trying to start their mission with the goal of failing fast?

We are all afraid of losses, pain, and embarrassment. Human beings do not like to experience such feelings. Ironically, these are exactly the same feelings associated with failure. One way of keeping away from the pain of failure is to avoid taking actions that have a high risk of leading to negative outcomes. However, leaders have to drive their organizations into the future. The future is always unknown and risky by nature. Therefore, leaders have no choice but to take risks. As a shortcut solution to this, leaders have been taught to hack their minds to believe that failing is a good thing. By setting failure as a goal, they are protecting themselves from feeling all the pain that comes after the inevitable failures.

Some take it to the next level and actually celebrate failure. This has been going on in the business world for over a decade now, and it is such a feel-good strategy that it has become extremely popular.

I have used the fail-fast methodology for many years in my personal and professional lives on dozens of critical projects. I used to believe in it very religiously. In the end, I concluded that it's not an effective approach because it gives you a false sense of progress and can be very costly in the long run without you realizing it. Just like alcohol and drugs numb people's pains, celebrating failure suppresses the real problem. I believe that this is a big mistake, and it's the root cause of many problems in society today because ...

When you start a journey with the expectation to fail, your first instinct is to accept roadblocks as failures and give up too fast or pivot rapidly to your next idea. As a result, you won't go as far as needed to experience your breakthroughs.

Never Look Forward to Failure, But ...

Don't get me wrong. I am not saying that failure is not important. What I am emphasizing is that we should not be looking forward to failure when starting any journey. It is extremely important to learn profoundly and learn fast from your failure so that you can grow to the next and better version of yourself.

Failing is painful, but it's even more painful when you don't learn and evolve from it.

We should definitely not be celebrating failure because by associating a positive feeling to it, we will not learn from it. We should be aiming and planning everything so that we succeed, but if and when failure comes, we should take the time to feel the pain and let it sink in. We need to experience the emotional pain of failure and then ask ourselves what we can learn from this. What could we have done better so that we know better for next time?

It is important to experience the pain of your failures. Learn deeply from them to earn your breakthroughs to the next level. It will make you stronger and wiser, faster.

In hindsight, the big failures that I faced at an early age taught me important lessons and shaped how I evolved in the next phase of my life. This has been a repetitive process leading to every major inflection point in my life so far. A lot of pain and struggles prior to earning my major leap forward.

While I was born a dreamer, I was not bold. For most of my childhood, I was extremely shy and afraid to talk to people about anything deep and meaningful. People did not respond positively to me because, at first impression, they thought I was dumb, unattractive, and a poor communicator. I did not have the courage to tell anyone about my big dreams, let alone pursue them. That is, until a couple of pivotal events took place in my teenage years, which taught me some of the most important lessons that shaped a very different future than expected for me.

These were major failures that I would have never looked forward to, nor would I wish it on anyone. However, when they happened, I accepted them and experienced the pain they brought and asked myself, "What can I learn from this?"

The first major transformational event took place when I was sixteen. I went mountain climbing and camping for the weekend with a group of my best friends in high school. It was summer vacation, and we joined a three-day summer program to climb one of the tallest and steepest mountains in Mauritius, called "Montagne Le Pouce." It was a great experience to climb all the way up to the top of the mountain using ropes and professional climbing gear. We were so proud to make it to the top of the mountain, and at sunset, we enjoyed breathtaking views of the entire island from coast to coast at a height of 2,600 feet.

It was my first time camping in the wilderness. We had a great time learning to set up a tent and camp overnight with the group. Over the next two days, we hiked and camped in different spots. On the third afternoon, we started our journey down to the base. This was one of the most memorable adventures of my life. I was carefree and walking around in sheer bliss. That is probably a terrible state of mind to be in while climbing down a mountain. For a moment, I ventured off the trail onto rocks leading to a major cliff that dropped straight to the base of the mountain. I wanted to get closer to the edge one last time to take in those amazing views.

I skipped a step and fell down on my back. The back of my head hit the rocky floor I was standing on. I lost consciousness and started slipping down. I tried to grab onto a plant that was nearby, but it immediately de-rooted, and I continued slipping down with the plant in my hands. I went into a daze, and I just let go, prepared to fall off the cliff. Surprisingly, I was not afraid of dying, and I completely let go of all worries and enjoyed the moment. Perhaps I remember it that way because I was barely conscious from the concussion.

Luckily a strong and agile friend had the reflex to hold on to a tree and grab me by the hair on my head in the nick of time. My friend pulled me back by my hair, and a few other people from our group joined him to get me back up to the trail. Thanks to him, I am still here today. We have unfortunately lost touch since high school. If you are reading this book, I would love to reconnect.

The second major transformational event happened when I was seventeen. My father was a very intelligent man. In fact, I would say he was a visionary. One day after he turned forty-four, he told us that he had a big dream and was going to do something monumental and different for the next chapter of his life. Unfortunately, that big mission he had to pursue was in another realm. My father got very sick, and his health rapidly disintegrated until he died from cancer six months later.

The six months when my father was sick was a very difficult time for all of us in the family. During this time, I got to spend a lot of time at home with my father, and I had no interest in attending high school. As a result, I failed the 12th-grade finals, which was one month after my father's funeral. In Mauritius, you cannot graduate high school and pursue higher education without passing the 12th-grade board examinations. Many may be shocked to learn that I never graduated high school, but it is my truth! Nonetheless, I somehow made it to a university across the world in the United States. That is a story for a different time.

These two back-to-back close encounters with death taught me the two most important lessons that were pivotal to how my life evolved from that point. It could have gone the other way and made me more fearful, shy, and risk-averse. I could have gone into depression, dealing with the trauma from these events. But luckily, I had the good judgment to ask myself, "What can I learn from this very difficult moment, and how do I need to evolve from here to build the best possible future?" The two lessons were as follows:

1. Life can be short, so I had to become impatient in pursuing my dream before it was too late. My father's sudden death taught me that we have no control over how long we live, so it gave me a sense of urgency to pursue the things I strongly believed in.

2. My circumstances led me to become bold and courageous to help my dear ones navigate through several bigger traumatic challenges that followed after my father's death. I learnt very quickly that in tough times, the best path forward is to give people strength by inspiring them with the vision of

a brighter future. The only purpose of revisiting the painful past is to learn important lessons from it so that you can build a more successful future. This was the moment when I knew that I wanted to become a great leader so that I could inspire more people to build a better world.

Fast-forward to twenty-five years later, I have learnt that the greater your dream, the more important it is for you to inspire many other capable and ambitious people to help you on your journey to your destination. That means leaders must be able to build a team that believes in their dream and is highly motivated to join them on their mission. It is very difficult to build and keep such a team when failure is the goal at the starting gate because people do not see failure as an inspiring outcome.

When success is the desired goal and wins are experienced right from the start of the journey, we not only attract and retain a talented and loyal team, but we are also more likely to attract other passionate stakeholders: partners, employees, customers, and investors—all the people you will need. In chapter 13, we explore how to build the "burn-on" team that is needed to succeed faster and win often instead of the typical "burnt-out" teams.

So far in this chapter, we have learned that the first step to succeed faster is to unlearn the fail-fast mindset. The next step to succeed faster is to …

Tap into the Zeitgeist

Is my idea going to be accepted by the market? Are my customers going to love my product? Will my innovative business be successful?

This is the billion-dollar question that every leader and dreamer wants answered before they venture into their big new project. In hindsight, it is easy to see through the winners from the losers, but when looking forward, it's very very hard to get it right consistently.

There are legendary stories and many more untold tales of startups that had great ideas with perfect execution and marketing, and in spite of the perfection, they failed badly. They failed because they didn't stand a chance to begin with, regardless of their effort and execution. The market simply wasn't ready to accept and embrace their idea. In other words, these ideas failed to tap into the zeitgeist.

The dictionary definition of the "zeitgeist" is: "the defining spirit or mood of a particular period of history as shown by the ideas and beliefs of the time."

Without alignment with the zeitgeist, it is nearly impossible to achieve success, regardless of how good your idea is and how bold your actions are.

Most leave it to luck and charge full speed ahead with the execution. The smarter approach is to invest some time studying the quality of your idea in comparison to the competitive landscape and focus on objectively understanding how good or bad your market timing is.

Out of the four possible market timing conditions, there are only two market timing strategies that can open the portal of the zeitgeist for you …

CHAPTER 1 – KEY TAKEAWAYS

YOUR NOTES

_____
_____
_____
_____
_____
_____
_____
_____
_____
_____
_____
_____
_____

Be a Seeker, Not a Bullshitter!

*Bullshitters go fast, into a wall.
Seekers start slow, but they end up
high and far, beyond the wall.*

CHAPTER 2

BE A SEEKER, NOT A BULLSHITTER!

know you want to hear more about the zeitgeist, but before we can learn how to tap into the zeitgeist, we need to address a very important prerequisite first. For the next eight secrets in this book to be effective, you need to make sure your mindset is tuned to,

Be a seeker and not a bullshitter.

In the past two decades, I have had the opportunity to lead many people and coach several business leaders. In my observation, the reason why even the most ambitious and hardest-working people struggle with success is not because of the lack of information and knowledge. In the digital era, information is at everybody's fingertips, and knowledge is a commodity that is easy to acquire for all. The problem is that ambitious people tend to have alpha personalities, and alphas are naturally predisposed to be overly optimistic, which earns them the reputation of a bullshitter.

The alphas are usually overflowing with confidence. They rarely doubt their ability to succeed at anything they undertake. They have a tendency to promote their ideas, and they mostly focus on the dreamy outcomes, causing them to miss out on important details about their goals. Alphas rarely pause to seek the truth that will help them determine the likelihood of success and the probability of failure prior to embarking on their mission.

In addition, the majority of people are followers of optimistic leaders. Follower personalities do not take the time to seek the truth about their goals because they tend to follow the path set by their alpha leaders. The followers are usually trying to copy the well-known, super-successful people. As established in the previous chapter, it is not wise to follow the 0.1 percent super successful because they have a special talent that is unique to them and not replicable by the rest of us.

Whether you are transforming your life, your career, a product, a service, or a business, innovation is what you need if you want to make significant progress.

The dichotomy of innovation is that it can be highly rewarding when done right and very punitive otherwise. You can be assured that there will be many roadblocks and risks on this journey because it is a novel path that has not been explored yet. Therefore, the personalities who take the lead to pursue their larger-than-life dreams need to have an unrealistic level of confidence and optimism, like the alpha personalities.

As a leader, you need to showcase a high level of confidence to inspire the customers, investors, and employees who are needed to accomplish your mission. Given the nature of innovation, many times, you will not have important answers figured out, and the facts will often be unknown until the end is near.

Innovation is uncertain by nature, and outcomes are never guaranteed. Therefore, bullshitting can be perceived as a useful

tool by many when navigating toward their goal—especially when the goal is to go fast instead of going far.

A better way of looking at it is you need ample optimism to show certainty about things that are actually uncertain and risky. If you project the facts, you will sound pessimistic. Why would anyone believe in you, join your company, invest money, and give you everything else you need to have your moonshot if you don't sound like you believe in it yourself?

An extreme adaptation of this philosophy is best captured in a mantra of success that was coined in the 1970s: "Fake it till you make it."

This controversial belief system led to the biggest economic crises of modern times with the dot-com bubble in the 1990s, followed by the subprime fraud that exploded with the great financial recession in 2008. During this period, some of the most sensational companies that rapidly rose to great heights eventually fell off a cliff when the public realized that their leaders were just faking it and that they would never be able to deliver on their dreamy promises. The founders and executive leaders of many such companies ended up in jail for committing the greatest large-scale business fraud of all time.

Enron, Bernie Madoff, Theranos, and FTX are a few examples. Such mega corporate scams, followed by unfortunate macroeconomic events, led to major pain in the economy. The millennial generation had a very difficult start in their careers during the first decade of this millennium, in spite of being the most highly educated generation in American history so far. This impacted that generation's future and was one of the main catalysts for the massive reshaping of modern culture that is still taking place.

Since "fake it till you make it" has caused so much disruption, we ought to study this notorious mindset so that we can learn and evolve from it.

The Bullshitter Mindset

Bullshitting comes very naturally to most leaders and those who follow them. The typical journey of bringing an innovative idea to market with the bullshitter mindset consists of the following three phases:

Phase 1: Dreaming

Phase 2: Execution

Phase 3: Promotion

The goal tends to be to get to the promotion phase as fast as possible. However, regardless of the stage, alphas carry a promoter mindset through all the three phases. They are always promoting. While promoting during the dreaming and promotion stage is beneficial, in the execution phase, it is a major liability. It will impair your intellectual honesty and blind you from foreseeing critical risks. Sooner or later, your credibility will be diminished to that of a bullshitter, and your chances of succeeding will be decimated.

Stumbling across major obstacles at the execution stage is the most popular cause for running out of funding and your mission not being able to make it to the finish line. Therefore, you want to avoid promotion during this stage because you are likely to be wrong and fail often. Over-optimism at this stage will impair your risk management skills, leading to irreparable damage.

There is a critical step missing between the dreaming and execution phase that can prevent the extremely high rate of failure through proper discovery and risk management. Since failure is the most likely outcome here, the leaders who subscribe to this process promote the idea that we should look forward to experiencing failure. "Failing fast is a good outcome" is what they have bullshitted us to believe!

Even if your mission was able to get through the execution phase alive, it is very likely to crash really fast in the promotion phase. The promotion phase is where you spread the word and let customers know about your product at scale. Good promoters have a significant advantage over others because they are able to scale out their product's awareness to a large group of people faster and cheaper than the rest. Even if you are the best promoter on the planet, what really matters in the end is:

Did the market get significant value from your product when they used it?

Did they fall in love with your product as soon as they experienced it?

Promoters are often so blinded by their optimism that they fail to notice when customers are not getting value from their product or when their product has a critical flaw that is leading to poor customer experience.

The dreamer and promoter mindsets are required to build innovative businesses, but it is only good when applied in the right doses, at the right time, and in the right place. Ninety percent of the deadly problems that surprise people in the execution and promotion phase could have been anticipated and avoided prior to these costly phases. In the end, the truth always prevails regardless of how great of a bullshit you promote. The later in the journey you become aware of the truth, the more painful and costly it is going to be.

As a rule of thumb, you have to pay for the rite of passage to success. Your only choice is to pay early or pay much more later. Which one will you choose?

Lessons Learned from a Reformed Bullshitter

I would have loved to tell you that I have never been a bullshitter in my entire life. Unfortunately, that is very far from the truth. Bullshitting is an art, one that I had mastered very well back in the day. One such example of where bullshitting led me to fail fast and fail hard was a few years before starting Techolution. I had an "amazing" business idea, named "HomeFellas," which was very innovative back then.

This idea was quite revolutionary for its time, and it stemmed from a personal problem I experienced. Also, I was very confident that millions of other people faced the same problem as me. During this time, my wife and I had just bought our first home, right as we welcomed our first child to this world, a baby boy. Very often, we would waste productive work and parenting time to find a suitable contractor and schedule appointments for repairs and renovations that were required.

The goal was to build the first mobile/Internet-based platform to enable homeowners to find suitable contractors, where they could then easily request pricing for comparison before hiring the best service provider within hours and without any site visits. Using this platform, homeowners could easily provide a detailed overview of the construction or repair job by clicking pictures and adding key information about their project with AI assistance from the HomeFellas app or website. This would enable contractors to rapidly review the project and submit their initial bid at the convenience of their smartphones. The homeowner could easily schedule a site visit directly from the calendar feature on our app right after reviewing the pricing. Our solution eliminated the friction from the selection process between homeowners and contractors.

My alpha personality trait led me to bullshit my way to convince my wife to invest our hard-earned savings, and I got a few friends to dedicate their personal time after their day jobs to build my vision. The HomeFellas team was sold in the early ideation stages. Without wasting any time researching my market and testing the viability of this idea, I jumped straight to execution. I spent my resources on hiring the right talent, managing, designing, and building the platform as a product owner and a lead software engineer.

The good news was that a few months after launching HomeFellas, we witnessed an overwhelming surge in demand on the customer front. Homeowners were grateful for this service, as I had anticipated. The bad news was that the business model failed, and it failed fast. I believed in the purpose of our company, and I committed to making this startup work so that I could comfortably exit my corporate job. Therefore, we started listening and learning fast about what both sides of the market really wanted. This led to several pivots and failures iteratively until I ran out of hope and cash.

I had assumed that if we were giving contractors free customer leads from the platform, they would jump on it for the business opportunity. In hindsight, this assumption was perhaps the single biggest mistake I made. While trying to pivot to make the business successful, contractors told me that they would only use the service if I offered them a phone-based virtual assistant with good computer knowledge to be the liaison between the website and them. In other words, the majority of the contractors were not ready to conduct business over the Internet because they were only comfortable with the phone.

Since I only related to the homeowners, I failed to understand the needs of the contractor. When I learnt that contractors would need a call-center-like service, I decided to abort the mission because I was sure that I only wanted to build an Internet/mobile-based business since that was where my expertise was and that is where the zeitgeist was going at the time. As luck would have it, many years later, I met an entrepreneur who made a fortune developing a very similar business model in the same time frame but targeting a more educated and brick-and-mortar market. His business was catering to people who were looking for doctors instead of contractors. Since doctor offices already had assistants with Internet-powered computers in 2008, they did not face the same overwhelming gaps to acquire the back-end consumer (contractors in my case, and doctors in theirs) of their platform. His business was super successful, and he cashed out big after selling his company.

In summary, my first startup didn't work because I failed to be a seeker. I bullshitted and built a business without really understanding the market that I was serving. Owning a smartphone and using the Internet on the go was not a mainstream thing before 2010, especially for construction workers. Since contractors were out at their job sites, they were not able to go on the Internet, even if they happened to be computer savvy. I did not take the time to understand the problem I was solving for my day 1 customers. I just jumped into the execution and promotion phase immediately after dreaming of the business idea. Had I sought the truth, I would have learned at the early ideation stage what I only ended up learning in hindsight, after failing and losing a few hundred thousand of dollars of my hard-earned money and countless personal and family time that I sacrificed and wasted. Building a platform is not as easy as it seems because there are two sides of the market that need to participate equally in order for the business model to work. In the case of HomeFellas, I needed to wow both the homeowner and the contractor.

While we wowed the homeowners, I was winging it (bullshitting) with the other critical customers, the contractors. Therefore, the HomeFellas business model failed!

The Missing Link

You will be surprised to hear that after all this bashing of the alphas, I believe that they are very important for evolutionary societies. Alphas tend to be pioneers, and with a little bit of luck on their side, they become great leaders. Their existing approach has most of the important ingredients needed to succeed, except for one! They are just missing a very special secret power tool. This secret tool will give them the superpower needed to succeed way more than they currently do with innovation.

It is time to introduce a seeking phase between the dreaming and the execution phase. When we have a dream that we feel very passionate about, instead of running to execute on it, we must take the time to seek the truth. Before building and promoting our dream, we need to objectively determine whether our day 1 customers, who represent our target market, are going to be wowed by our idea. We need to assess the viability of our idea as objectively as possible before making a commitment. This is done through meticulous research, simulation, and risk planning very early in the process.

Jumping straight into the seeking phase is also not very effective to find the truth that you need to know in order to succeed.

Most go through the seeking process, and they still miss the truth in plain sight because they are blinded by the love for their

dream, the excitement of a bright future, and the assumption of success being the default outcome.

Remember that success isn't the default. Failure is the default state of things in life. Do nothing, and failure is guaranteed, with the exception of the rare lottery winners. Technically, they still have to buy the lottery to win! That is why you must adjust your mindset to always be seeking the truth for the purpose of accomplishing something great faster and smoother because in the end, after all the distractions and fanfare, only the truth will prevail. Therefore, before starting the seeking phase, you need to transform to the seeker mindset.

With this mindset, your only goal is to find the knowable truth you need to know in order to get to your end goal, regardless of how heartbreaking it may be. Remember, it is always better to pay early than to pay much more later. Because your goal now is to find the truth sooner and shatter your dreams as early in the game as possible if you happen to be on the wrong path. The seeker mindset will help you fight the infamous confirmation bias that sneaks its way from your heart into your mind when you are in the honeymoon phase of any new idea you have fallen in love with. This explains why they say love is blind.

The Four Phases of the Succeed-Faster Journey

Four Phases of the Succeed-Faster Journey

The seeking phase is where you are required to actively practice the seeker mindset to find the truth about whether your dream has the potential to achieve the success that you believe it does. I would strongly suggest to embrace the seeker mindset in your core all the time, regardless of which phase you are going through.

You can learn every day from your mistakes after they happen. You can learn for entertainment, or you can learn for years through a formal institution with a vague and long-term purpose of becoming more educated and skilled. Learning is great, and I would encourage it. However, when you are on a mission to accomplish a specific goal, seeking is the most effective at improving your probability and speed of success.

Seeking is different from learning. Learning is broad and may not have a specific purpose. But seeking is looking for the truth that you need to understand in order to accomplish your specific mission as effectively as possible.

A seeker only focuses on learning what they need to know in order to get to their destination. They meticulously go seek the truth to ensure the right decisions and take the right actions. This alone will accelerate and improve the quality of your journey toward success.

It is easy to preach in a book to adopt a seeker mindset, but real life is a lot more nuanced. If you were always thinking about the truth, that might make you analytical and pessimistic. However, to the outside world, you still have to be the highly confident person that you are to inspire them to join your mission.

The Solution

Adopt and project whatever personality is necessary to get the job required done at any given time. Embrace the dreamer personality when you are in the process of ideating. Be a "bad-ass" executor personality with a "get things done" approach when you are in the execution phase. Embody the promoter personality like the best promoters in the world when in the promotion phase, pitching to investors, hiring a team, and reaching out to customers.

However, with yourself and with your trusted inner circle, you must recalibrate your mindset from the bullshitter mindset to a seeker mindset on an ongoing basis. This can be very difficult, but it is a necessity if you want to stop failing again and again on your journey to success. The first practical step is to remind yourself of this one absolute fact on this planet:

There are no guarantees in life. There are only probabilities.

So, no matter what you do, you can only impact the probability of achieving what you desire. Embracing this fact of life will liberate you from stressing about outcomes on a daily basis. Only focus on your decisions and actions.

Are you seeking what are the right decisions to make next?

Are you taking the right actions on a daily basis?

Is the quality of your daily decisions and actions leaping you toward your end goal?

If you have a promoter personality with a naturally optimistic outlook on things, it may be hard to change it to the more realistic and balanced mindset of a seeker. There is a simple but highly effective exercise to help you make the evolution to the seeker mindset. Every morning, when you begin your day and before you make decisions or take actions, follow this two-step process:

Step 1: Write "I am a seeker, not a bullshitter!" on a piece of paper, and read it aloud.

Step 2: Repeat the above nine more times.

In addition, whenever you catch yourself drifting into an overly dreamy or promotional mood, take a one-minute pause, and practice this exercise before making any decisions and taking action.

CHAPTER 2 – KEY TAKEAWAYS

Before

Dreaming Phase	Execution Phase	Promotion Phase
Dreamer Personality	Executor Personality	Promoter Personality
Bullshitter Mindset	Bullshitter Mindset	Bullshitter Mindset

Be a Seeker, Not a Bullshitter!

Dreaming Phase	Seeker Phase	Execution Phase	Promotion Phase
Dreamer Personality	Seeker Personality	Executor Personality	Promoter Personality
Seeker Mindset	Seeker Mindset	Seeker Mindset	Seeker Mindset

YOUR NOTES

_____

_____

_____

_____

_____

_____

_____

_____

_____

_____

_____

_____

_____

Succeed Faster **SECRET #3**

Tap into the Zeitgeist!

to significantly improve your luck with building your business idea. You will succeed faster by aligning yourself with the extremely powerful market forces of the zeitgeist before deciding what to build.

CHAPTER 3

TAPPING INTO THE ZEITGEIST

Market timing is single-handedly the most important factor that determines whether your big idea will be successful, super successful, or another failure. There are several factors that need to come together to build a great company, such as team skills, attitude, motivation, funding, and the quality of execution. However, aligning with the extremely powerful market forces, the zeitgeist is the most effective way to succeed faster. From my experience, there is no question that tapping into the zeitgeist is by far the most important ingredient for success.

Before we get too deep into why aligning with the extremely powerful market forces is important, let's revisit the formal dictionary definition of "zeitgeist":

ZEITGEIST

"The defining spirit or mood of a particular period of history as shown by the ideas and beliefs of the time."

Tapping into the Zeitgeist

Have you ever felt at some point in your life that your colleagues or competitors were much more successful than you, even though they were less skilled and hardworking?

When someone's career or business idea is in lockstep with the market trends without them being intentional about it, we call that "luck." If you ever felt that someone's skills, education, and competency don't add up to their success, then you just witnessed luck at play. They must have unintentionally experienced the magic of the zeitgeist. The saying "being at the right place at the right time" is in full effect here. For many successful people, it may be pure coincidence that they had the right idea and were at the right place with perfect timing. However, only a select few high achievers are intentional about their success and can repeat their accomplishments, because they carefully research and calculate their next move to ensure alignment with the zeitgeist.

What if there was a way to decode luck? What if you also had access to the same secrets to success as the select few achievers who can repeat their wins?

The Research

Let me tell you about one of the most interesting research studies conducted in this space on thousands of businesses that indicate that market timing is the most important factor for the success of a new product/service being launched. One such study was conducted by Bill Gross of Idealab.[4] This research study examined hundreds of startups that the company's Venture Funds had invested in over the years. It analyzed the correlation of five key attributes to determine which one had the most significant impact on the success or failure of these businesses.

---

4   Chris Dessi, "5 Top Indicators for Startup Success, According to This TED Talk: The biggest reasons why startups succeed today," accessed November 20, 2023, https://www.inc.com/chris-dessi/this-ted-talk-explains-the-5-reasons-why-startups-succeed.html.

In this study, they looked at the "usual suspect" factors, including the team's strength, business idea, funding, business model, and market timing to learn what successful startups had in common. Surprisingly to the sponsors of this research, it wasn't the team's strength or the end product's quality that predicted success most accurately.

It was whether the product being brought to market aligned with the customer's urgency and awareness at the time of launch. In other words, market timing!

The research study concluded that market timing contributed around 42 percent toward the business's success, with the strength of the founding team coming in second at 32 percent. Quality of the idea contributed around 28 percent, followed by the business model at 24 percent, and surprisingly, the least important factor was funding at a mere 14 percent.

The Four Types of Market Timing Conditions

I hope by now I have presented a compelling argument for the merit of an audacious and controversial statement made in the previous chapter:

Without alignment with the zeitgeist, it is nearly impossible to achieve success regardless of your big dreams and bold actions.

Therefore, you must make the commitment to always study where your idea lies on the zeitgeist spectrum before indulging in the execution phase. Ideas that align with certain market timing conditions are the only ones that can open the zeitgeist portal for you. In chapter 7, we dive deeper into the two "winning" market timing strategies. We will also introduce you to a zeitgeist predictive model that reveals how closely your business idea aligns with the powerful market forces, offering insight into your probability of success. For now, I would like to introduce you to the following:

The Market Timing Quadrant

At the end of chapter 7, you will find a detachable version of the Zeitgeist Predictive Matrix along with a Zeitgeist worksheet to help you assess where your product or service idea falls on the market timing spectrum.

#1 GREENFIELD MARKET — "THE ZEITGEIST"

A **Greenfield market** timing condition occurs when the demand for a product or service closely representing yours ranges from high to very high, while the supply/competition is significantly lower. Unfortunately, this favorable circumstance does not often occur in today's overly populated, highly educated, and hyper-globalized world. The Greenfield market, also known as "the Zeitgeist," is always hiding in plain sight, like a needle in a haystack, along with all the fads of its time.

When your dream aligns perfectly with the spirit and mood of the era, your odds of winning are significantly higher before you even get started. If your idea is executed and brought to market when the mood is in a new transition and the market is just getting ready to accept your offering, we call it "perfect" market timing.

A good example of a Greenfield market timing condition was the e-commerce/online retail industry in the late 1990s and early 2000s. Amazon and eBay were quintessential zeitgeist market timing strategies that made it big from the Greenfield market opportunity. There are very few other winners in this market category that still stand strong on their own. This is because most other players that tapped into the zeitgeist in the e-commerce space in that era have been acquired for hundreds of millions (diaper.com by Amazon) to a few billion dollars (Zappos by Amazon).

Apple's iPhone is probably going to be one of the best-known and most impactful zeitgeist market timing strategies of our time. More about this in the zeitgeist case study section later in this chapter.

Once in a while, Greenfield market opportunities present themselves discreetly but are ready to benefit those who are paying attention. We will explore how to find and capitalize on such opportunities in chapter 7.

Tapping into the zeitgeist is undoubtedly the winning market timing strategy.

This window of opportunity is usually very short where demand is rising rapidly and supply is very limited because only a select few have the competitive advantage and technical know-how to capitalize on this golden gap in the market. Once the zeitgeist becomes clearly visible to everyone and the competitive advantage becomes common knowledge, it is usually too late

to take advantage of the abundance of the golden gap because the market suddenly becomes very competitive or "Redfield."

#2 REDFIELD MARKET—"THE DISRUPTOR"

The majority of leaders and so-called innovators like to play it safe because of their fear of failure. As a result, they end up waiting too long to execute their dreams in spite of being aware that their idea is very likely aligned with the zeitgeist.

This phenomenon happens because it is nearly impossible to know for sure whether you have tapped into the zeitgeist, unless you have the right tools!

When the demand for a product/service is booming, you are likely going to face intense competition because others are also aware of the positive developments in the industry. Even though you are in a growth market, the demand is almost always counterbalanced by a rapid influx of competitors on the supply side. While competition is very good for customers, it is bad for people launching a new product/ service and investors backing those businesses because they face the wrath of a **Redfield market**.

In short, we call it a Redfield market timing when demand is high and growing and supply is also following the same course. In this type of market, you can only become a successful disruptor if your solution deeply connects with the key pain points of your customers. Your approach should also be uniquely different from that of the established competitors.

Google is a quintessential example of a market disruptor that entered a Redfield market in the late 1990s. Their unique approach helped them grab market share away from all the established competitors in the crowded search engine space at the time. Over the past twenty years, Google has been able to successfully capture all the growth in demand. As a result, they are virtually a monopoly in the search engine industry and have made it to the list of top ten richest companies worldwide, with $1.34 trillion market capitalization.

Whether Google will continue to maintain its monopoly as a search engine platform after the advent of novel AI technologies like ChatGPT remains to be seen. In chapter 7, we will unpack Google's remarkable case study as the disruptor in a Redfield market condition.

Redfield markets are a lucrative proposition despite the risk of intense competition because you can build a successful business faster by learning from the mistakes made by those who came before you. Also, you don't need to work so hard to create market awareness as the pioneers have already laid the foundation. On the flip side, you have to be amazing at execution because of the cutthroat competition that prevails in this type of market.

#3 BROWNFIELD MARKET— "LONG-TERM POTENTIAL"

Being early with your market timing in an industry with growing demand is a smart strategy. However, being too early could also mean that the growth in demand may be transient and not quite established. With low and unpredictable future market demand, scaling your business to escape velocity level within your allotted runway can be very difficult.

We call it a **Brownfield market** when the level of demand is low to medium but not really established yet. On the other hand, the supply is usually nonexistent because the market is very speculative and quite challenging to break into from a technical standpoint.

Many markets remain Brownfield for extended periods because of the lack of supply of a viable solution that the market is impatiently waiting for. Perhaps a major technical advancement is awaited, which relies on a few pioneers investing in unpredictable and expensive research and development projects. For example, a pollution-free and 100 percent renewable car and home power solution have remained a Brownfield market for decades because of the lack of viable solutions and the technical complexity involved.

In other cases, people may have achieved the scientific breakthrough, but the ecosystem needed to go to market may not be ready to support them.

General Magic is my favorite example of a player who entered a Brownfield market and failed because of the immaturity of their partner ecosystem. More about General Magic in the case study section of this chapter because they are the most impactful best-kept secret of modern times.

It is important to note that Brownfield markets can occasionally turn into a Greenfield one. The participants that play in the Brownfield market can develop significant competitive advantage. However, it is rare for the companies that break through Brownfield markets to last long enough for financial reasons to take advantage of the zeitgeist when the golden gap appears. Therefore, the Brownfield market play is only for the passionate few who can afford to lose everything for the cause they believe in. In chapter 7, we will explore further on how to handle this specific market condition because it has to be either avoided or handled with great care.

Figure—Golden Gap Concept

#4 DEADFIELD MARKET—"STAY AWAY"

The name "**Deadfield**" is very suggestive of what this market holds for people. Death is inevitable in this type of market condition. The question is not "if" but rather "when" the market will be dead. In this market, the demand for a particular product/service is falling consistently from a high to a medium level. However, the supply remains high as many established competitors are already in the field.

In the early stages of a Deadfield market, the participants do not realize that they have entered a dying sector. They hope for divine intervention and a miraculous turnaround. In more advanced stages, the market participants hesitate to leave because of their sunk cost and the ease of continuing to engage in a game they know very well.

The video cassette and DVD rental market in the 2000s is a prime example of Deadfield market timing. In the mid-2000s, the explosion of online video streaming services like YouTube and Netflix caused the video DVD and cassette rental industry to quickly turn what was a Redfield market into a Deadfield market. This led to the rapid demise of prominent players in the industry, such as Blockbuster and Hollywood Video among a multitude of others.

Even a formidable new player like Redbox failed to escape the fate of entering a Deadfield market, in spite of their cost-effective approach to serving customers and being fully backed by the fast-food giant McDonald's. We will explore this intriguing case study further in chapter 7.

Deadfield markets are very risky. I advise staying far away from investing and executing ideas that fall in this type of market timing condition.

The Zeitgeist Case Study

Now it's time to dive deeper into two related but highly contrasting case studies, where one was too early for the market (Brownfield timing), and its successor managed to tap into the zeitgeist with absolutely perfect market timing. This is the story of iconic Steve Jobs launching the iPhone and the contrasting tale of General Magic, Silicon Valley's best-kept secret.

Once upon a time, before touch-based smartphones became a reality, there were several innovations that led up to their development. The first-generation mobile flip phones that came to the market allowed users to only make phone calls on the go. After some more research and development, the keyboard-based Personal Data Assistants (PDAs) came into existence. This new version was far more dynamic than its predecessors as it allowed users to send and receive emails, manage their calendar appointments, and do much more from a pocket-sized device. It was considered a very innovative but niche technology until 2007, when Steve Jobs introduced a magical device named the iPhone.

Speaking of magic, that's precisely what a spin-off of the technology giant Apple created. In 1990, there were no digital mobile phones and certainly none with the World Wide Web accessible on the go. However, a group that operated in near-complete secrecy, known as General Magic, had a futuristic vision and determination to make portable smartphones a reality. They wanted to develop what would ultimately become a pocket-sized "handheld computer" and even envisioned it being small enough to wear on your wrist, just like a watch.

General Magic is a company most of you have never heard of because it does not exist anymore. However, during the 1990s, it was among the most exciting startups that also established the cornerstone for modern-age innovations. Although it may not be entirely appropriate to draw parallels, the level of innovation achieved by General Magic at the time is comparable to that of today's revolutionary OpenAI technology.

Originally, General Magic started as a project led by a team of techies within the Apple organization. However, when the team struggled to obtain resources and leeway to move their grandiose dream forward, it was spun off as an independent entity with the blessing of Apple's CEO John Sculley, Steve Jobs's successor after he was abruptly fired in 1985.

General Magic enjoyed some initial success, attracting millions of dollars in investment money and forming partnerships with major telecommunication giants. In 1995, it became Silicon Valley's first company with zero revenue to launch an Initial Public Offering (IPO). The term "Concept IPO" was coined after General Magic accomplished this feat.

Although the group achieved several epic-scale technical breakthroughs early on, the idea failed to work cohesively as the initial product they had envisioned. As a result, General Magic's team was not able to launch a viable product, and they also failed to generate enough revenue to sustain operations. Unfortunately, the company was eventually dissolved in 2004. At this point, you must be wondering what led to the downfall of such a pioneer in the tech industry.

There are several reasons for General Magic's demise. Despite having some of the smartest minds on their team, a larger-than-life dream, and nearly unlimited funding, General Magic's end product was a flop. They failed to execute on their wow factor before running out of funds because of a lack of focus (more about this in chapter 7).

General Magic also entered a Brownfield market that was way ahead of its time! Even if they had executed on their idea perfectly, the odds of succeeding were close to zero, to begin with. The market ecosystem of suppliers (i.e., parts manufacturers) and distribution partners (i.e., cellular network infrastructure) they needed to succeed weren't ready to support their grandiose dream. They failed to reach escape velocity before running out of their runway. This is the typical fate of players who dare to enter the Brownfield market.

While they were not able to succeed as a business, they certainly lived up to their name. Their inventions were no less than magical. The innovations pioneered at General Magic eventually evolved into technologies that we cannot live without today. This includes mobile touchscreens, USB ports, software modems, voice recognition, networked games, streaming television, programming that allows different mobile brands to communicate with one another, rich multimedia email that turns plain text into robust messages, and early versions of e-commerce.

Many key players of General Magic continue to be authoritative figures in the tech industry as founders or core team members associated with household brands like eBay, Android, Google, and Nest.

For Apple, their investment wasn't all lost because Steve Jobs built the iPhone on the foundation of General Magic to tap into the zeitgeist of the new millennia. Steve Jobs was especially known for his vision and ability to execute great products with extreme focus. As for market timing, I think it would be fair to say that he knew how to tap into the zeitgeist because he did it over and over again during his nearly four-decades-long career!

Steve Jobs understood the difference between people's "needs" and their "wants." He delivered something that met those wants in such a profound way that today his products have transitioned from "want" to "need." Steve Jobs, and the iPhone, is an example of someone who turned a Brownfield market into a Greenfield one. Mr. Jobs's excellent execution ability combined with his celebrity status helped to generate significant initial demand for the iPhone.

All things considered, it is undeniable that the market timing was on Steve Jobs's side when the iPhone launched because, at this point, all the market forces were cooperating and ready. For example, the cellular mobile infrastructure that the iPhone required to be a phone was much more mature, and the parts manufacturer ecosystem was readily available to support the rapid manufacturing of the iPhone, unlike what General Magic had to face during their era.

Significant Evolution over Drastic Revolution

While revolutions are necessary for significant radical changes once in a while, there is no denying that they come at a great cost. As we have seen with the General Magic case study, what they attempted was nothing less than a revolution of computer technology of its era. It established the foundation for the world's future but, unfortunately, led to the painful failure of General Magic as a company.

Contrary to popular belief, what Steve Jobs attempted with the iPhone cannot be considered a drastic revolution. Now you know your history from the case study in this chapter. The iPhone was a significant evolution of the mobile phone and personal computer technology based on the foundation already established by General Magic's failed revolution. As a result, the iPhone made Apple the most valuable company in the world. This paved the way for today's smartphones and mobile "personal computers" that are far more available and affordable, transforming how people work, transact, and socialize worldwide. The barrier for anyone to move up the ladder and do well in life is the lowest it has ever been in the history of humankind.

Imagine what the world would have been like if the novel coronavirus (COVID-19) had occurred in the late 1900s without today's technologies. Back then, we would not have been able to stay connected and work and transact 24/7 while we were forced to be physically isolated because of the pandemic.

I know for me and my mom, videoconferencing made a big difference during the pandemic. She lives in Mauritius, over 10,000 miles from the United States, almost on the other side of the planet. As a social person who enjoys getting out and socializing, being confined at home alone became very depressing for my mom. Fortunately, technology enabled her to talk and see to her children and grandchildren, especially my newborn child, whom she did not physically meet till he was three years old. Every Sunday morning, I would FaceTime (videoconference) with her from my home or car. She was able to see my newborn grow. She also got to experience his first smile, his first words, and his first walk. It's as if she was here with us the whole time without physically being here. That helped keep my mom's spirits up in spite of the global lockdown.

This is the level of impact zeitgeist can have on society and our lives. But unfortunately, major innovations that can enhance our lives can be unpredictable and inconsistent. Sometimes it takes just a few years for major advancements, and sometimes it can take a century to become useful for everyone.

For instance, the concept of videoconferencing dates back to the 1870s but did not become a reality until the personal computer revolution in the early 1980s. Thanks to visionaries like Steve Jobs, videoconferencing has been available to the mainstream population since the launch of the FaceTime feature on the iPhone. People across the globe can see and talk to one another in real time from anywhere for free! This would be considered nothing less than pure magic if you told someone about it just a century ago.

There are many other similar instances where one ambitious dreamer failed to tap into the zeitgeist of their era, but in a future period, a successor evolved the failed invention to achieve massive commercial success. For instance, the electric car did not go mainstream until recently, even though it was pioneered in the 1800s. The early electric car entrepreneurs were visionaries like General Magic, with their own failed revolutions. However, they did not have the zeitgeist on their side like Elon Musk did with the Tesla venture. Tesla will go down in history for significantly advancing the adoption of electric cars in the mainstream.

Predicting the Zeitgeist of Our Era?

While today's technologies seem to have us pretty well covered, there are plenty of problems that we have yet to solve for, which will likely present new opportunities. Just imagine what we can build today based on yesterday's failed innovation to shape tomorrow!

Predicting the zeitgeist can be as tricky as accurately forecasting an earthquake! We can only be certain after it has started. I have no way of guessing the zeitgeist in advance other than using the Zeitgeist Predictive Model (chapter 7). So I can only share my speculative opinion on some of the areas where I believe the zeitgeist of our era will come from.

Over the last century, we have seen a rapid boom in innovation and technology that has bettered the existence of the human race on this planet in a magnificent way. Mobility has become more possible across the lands, the oceans, the skies, and even space. Also, progression in financial status and social class within a short span of time has become more accessible to all. Information is widely available to everyone, and our civilization is doing much better than ever before.

All this rapid innovation has also been a double-edged sword. Everyday issues have taken a chaotic twist and turned into major problems that impact humanity as a whole. Some of the recent unsolved issues of our times are the pandemic, civil unrest, major inequality gaps, healthcare accessibility, social network manipulation, technology-controlled culture, hyperinflation, labor shortage, inequality gaps, climate change leaving our planet uninhabitable, and how AI impacts society in the years ahead. While these larger-than-life problems are very troubling, they are also exciting opportunities for dreamers to evolve our world to a version that we would all want to live in.

The transformations that could solve the problems of our times and positively impact the quality of life on this planet are where the zeitgeist of our times lies.

As the world becomes more sophisticated, will technologies like AI control us? Or will it enable us to live more meaningful lives?

It's the ambitious leaders, entrepreneurs, and intrapreneurs who will determine the ultimate outcome. The future is a blank canvas, and it will be dreamers like us who will paint the picture of tomorrow.

For that we must understand what people will need in the next window of opportunity and then deliver it as fast and effectively as possible.

In other words, we need to become really good at tapping into the zeitgeist!

CHAPTER 3 – KEY TAKEAWAYS

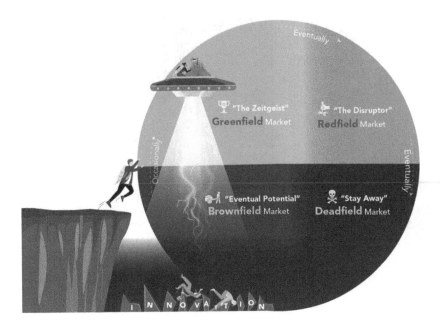

YOUR NOTES

MY PERSONAL EXPERIENCE WITH THE ZEITGEIST

nadvertently had my first experience with the zeitgeist at the young age of fifteen. However, the concept of the zeitgeist would not come into my awareness until two decades later. At this age, I believed that the only thing needed to succeed was my God-given gift of dreaming big and doing bold. I was born with the personality of a dreamer, and I was developing the skills of a promoter, but I surely didn't have the seeker mindset yet.

In hindsight, I can unequivocally say that being part of the zeitgeist was the number one factor why someone like me, who was born average or arguably below average, is where I am today. I owe my gratitude for experiencing the zeitgeist at an early age to the first master of the zeitgeist that I ever met, my father.

I grew up in a middle-class family on a small island in Africa called Mauritius. Although small in size, the beautiful and diverse natural landscapes make this island look nothing less than paradise. Life in

Mauritius was all about working hard to get a good education, earn a living, and spend free time cherishing simple things like socializing with the extended family, relishing the unique but delicious cuisine, playing soccer, enjoying the beach, and exploring the beautiful mountainous nature.

Back when I was growing up, we had an amazing and free education system from kindergarten to twelfth grade. However, Mauritius didn't have a university. Therefore, anyone who wanted to pursue higher education had to go abroad. Due to the lower cost of living, it was a big deal for parents to send their children to faraway foreign places with reputable higher education, such as the United Kingdom, France, and the United States. Ever since I can remember, I didn't know why and how, but I always knew that I would go to America when I grew up.

In elementary school, I grew a fascination with the game of soccer, and my dream was to become a soccer star playing in the English Premier League. The English Premier League is very popular in Mauritius because of its colonial history, and to date, the locals fanatically follow the sport. I used to imagine myself on the field, making amazing dribbles and scoring goals. Although I was great at soccer in my eyes and used to imagine myself dribbling like Pelé, I didn't even make the cut to play for my high school team. Actually, I did make the team one season because of my persistence. I convinced the coach to give me a chance, and he eventually gave me a shot. I ended up sitting on the bench at all the games because the coach felt that I didn't have the physical stature and strength for my age group to play at this level. Especially that I didn't like to pass and my go-to strategy on the field was to dribble.

After sitting on the bench for a couple of seasons at the most prestigious stadiums in Mauritius, I was starting to get bored and frustrated. When it became clear that I was not going to get very far with playing for my high school, let alone the English Premier League, I was committed to find a new dream for my future. I pivoted to my next area of fascination, air travel. I wanted to be an airline pilot. This dream did not last long after my father came to know about my newfound career plan. In no uncertain terms, he told me that he wasn't going to pay a fortune to send me to the United States to become an airplane pilot.

Over time, I grew interested in the engineering of useful technologies like the airplane, automobile, and electronics. I was always very intrigued by how the giant aircrafts worked and what it took for them to fly at such great heights, above the tall mountain peaks and the soaring skyscrapers. I used to befriend car mechanics so that I could open the bonnet of a car and learn about how cars worked. My curiosity for electricity and electronics was very high. Whenever contractors visited my home or my father's small pharmacy store, I would assist them to learn how they worked, especially electricians. I asked them all sorts of questions and even played with the electrical equipment and the car parts at home.

Back then, I broke more stuff than I fixed, but my father never raised any questions or scolded me for this, even though he was strict otherwise. He always encouraged my curiosity and scientifically minded brain. At the age of fourteen, I remember being very interested in assembling my own computer. At that time, very few people had computer systems at home. You had to configure your own computer and pay a professional to assemble it. My father bought me all the parts that I asked for, even though we lived on a tight budget, and there was a high chance I would break something while assembling my first computer with a modem to connect to the Internet.

Having a personal computer was a luxury most other kids in my era didn't have, and we definitely did not have discretionary money to spend. Nonetheless, my father being a forward thinker with a pragmatic approach to things in life fully enabled my first adventure with innovation. In 1995, I was one of the first hundred people in Mauritius to connect to the Internet with the good old dial-up modem going, "Pshhhkkkkkkrrrrkakingkakingkakingtshchchchchchchchcch *ding*ding*ding*."

One evening at the family dining table, I was telling my mother that I wanted to go to the United States to study aeronautical engineering at a university so that I could build airplanes. My mother was so excited about the idea, but on the other hand, my father laughed. He said, "That's great, but when you return to Mauritius after your studies, you will not have a job in this country because there aren't any companies building planes here. They only need a few qualified engineers to fix and maintain Air Mauritius's fleet of airplanes." One more time, my father asked me to stop dreaming about majors to study that wouldn't have a return on investment.

So out of frustration, I said, "You keep on telling me no, so why don't you tell me what field of higher education studies you will approve of?" Finally, after years of hearing no, my father revealed that he was going to take on the burden of funding my expensive American education only if I studied computers. So I said, OK, I'll be a computer engineer because I actually enjoy building computers! I thought that would seal the deal, but I was very disappointed when my father turned down computer engineering. Out of frustration, I yelled, "You just said yes to computer studies, but now you are saying no to computer engineering. Just tell me what exactly you want me to do!" He was very specific. With conviction, my father told me

74

that the only degree he would approve of was Computer Science. My response was, "Computer what?"

Although computer science, also known as software engineering, has existed as a branch of computer technology since the 1960s, it was a very Brownfield market until the late 1990s. During that time, computers used to be large, clunky machines that occupied a lot of space, unlike modern-age smart devices that you can fit in your pockets. Software development was a relatively new field with limited capabilities. Therefore, software engineering wasn't a well-known profession during the early 1990s. I took a Fortran and Pascal programming class in high school and hated it with passion. The rebel inside me had taken over, and I questioned how my father was making such predictions about the future when he had never even used a computer, let alone working with software!

My father was born into a family with nine siblings, and his father owned a small garment store in Mauritius. He was a pharmacist by profession and didn't know any computer or software engineers.

His closest encounter with a computer was a scientific calculator that he used very proficiently to tally up the books for his small pharmacy store in Mauritius. I thought that my father was just being difficult to discourage me from going abroad for higher education when he got so specific with what degree he would allow me to study in the United States. In my head, I was like, "What's the difference if I pursue computer science or computer engineering? It's pretty much the same in terms of return on investment, so let me do what I like."

Life took an unexpected turn in 1996 when my father sadly lost his life after bravely fighting cancer for six months. This tragedy happened around the time of my 12th-grade board exams. This is a very important exam in Mauritius, and without passing it, one does not graduate high school. With everything going on at home, studying for my 12th-grade finals was the last thing on my mind. This was an important turning point in my life, and the next unpredictable moves I made set me on the path that led to where I am today.

Against the will of my mother and other elders in my extended family, I decided to skip high school and spent time helping my mother and my siblings through this very difficult transition period. I took a full-time job as a computer technician at a local computer store. They gave me a company van, and I drove to large corporate client offices to install computers and servers. I also connected their local area network with the Internet through the first generation of modems.

I somehow held on to my dream of going to the United States for higher education, even though all my cards were stacking up against that possibility. At lunchtime and after work, I would spend a considerable amount of time at the US Consulate in Mauritius. I was such a regular there that the American lady in charge of the office became my friend. From here, I learnt the steps I needed to take to get into a decent low-cost university in the United States.

My mother was very supportive of me following my passion, and she loved the idea of her kids getting the best higher education possible. My mother and my sister ran my father's pharmacy and garment store so that they could make enough money to support the family.

However, with the sudden turn of events, my mother wasn't sure how she would finance the costly university fees in the United States. One day, I asked my mother to accompany me to the US Consulate office. As she walked in, the lady in charge of the consulate greeted my mother and told her, "I am tired of seeing your son visit this office. You need to send him to study in the US. Don't worry, he will do great over there."

My mother was impressed at how I was able to get this person of higher authority to tell her this. She decided to take a leap of faith. My mother worked really hard and scraped whatever money she could to pay for my college fees in the United States. I will always be indebted to her for the sacrifices she had to make in order to support me and my siblings after my father passed away.

In 1997, I finally flew to the United States and enrolled into college to study computer engineering. I was now living my dream. Even though life was not easy during this time, it was the most optimistic and happiest period of my life. The moment I got to the United States, I started looking for part-time jobs to help pay for my living expenses while my mother paid the major college tuition fees. My first job was as a desk attendant at one of the dormitories in college. I worked the night shifts on the weekends to make whatever extra money I could, as they paid 50 percent more for this shift. I started hustling to find more work opportunities to make more money as my younger brother was getting ready to go to college.

My skills in assembling computers and setting up Internet modems became very useful. I got a part-time gig that had decent pay for those times. I made $9 an hour assembling and fixing computers on campus! To give you some context, the average minimum wage at the time was $4 an hour, and this wasn't even a full-time job. The reason why I was paid almost double the minimum wage was because I knew how to assemble computers, work with modems, and connect them to the Internet. Thanks to my father, who never turned down my request to learn something new, especially when it came to computers and the Internet.

This job kept me busy as the university was giving every new student and every faculty member an Internet-enabled computer. During the three-month-long summer break, I didn't have enough money to go back to Mauritius, so I stayed back on the deserted campus and worked full-time at the computer lab. I was on call to fix computers and Internet problems for the permanent administrative staff and the few professors who were on the campus teaching summer classes.

Sometimes this job led me to some very interesting discoveries about the most powerful people on campus. One summer morning, I was sent to the office of the president of my university to fix a problem with his Internet. The gentleman was probably in his late sixties or early seventies. He was very kind to me. He logged me into his computer and opened Netscape, the most popular Internet browser back then, and showed how his Internet wasn't working.

As I was troubleshooting his problem, I unintentionally came across his search history, and the websites I saw in that list were not what I would expect from someone this important to do on his work computer at the workplace. He did have a large private office, and I know you must be very curious to know what happened behind the closed doors of the university's president office, but I'll leave that to your imagination.

The thought of leveraging this secret to correct my low GPA crossed my mind, but my good upbringing kicked in, and I didn't even confront the person. I deleted his browser history without being asked to do so.

In addition to the interesting side job that I was doing on campus, I was thoroughly enjoying the computer engineering classes I had to take, including Assembly, Physics, and Electronics 101. For two whole years, I witnessed my senior friends who were in the computer science program get full-time jobs paying $80,000 to $90,000 before graduating. A starting salary of $80,000 in 1999 is worth $160,000 today. It is unheard of for college grads to make this type of starting salary even to this date. This is when it hit me that my father had foreseen something that most people didn't. I immediately switched my major to computer science and started to actively learn coding and got my hands on as many software development projects as I could on campus.

Soon my campus jobs went from hardware to getting paid $15 an hour to automate the conversion of the college course catalog from a rich text file to the HTML and Javascript-based website. I got so good at solving software problems in Java, HTML, and Javascript that I landed a job paying $17/hour in 1999 to teach faculty members how to convert all their coursework into an HTML website. I was getting paid an unheard amount of money as an international student to basically teach my teachers how to transition to the first generation of online teaching.

Switching my majors to computer science was a calculated move, and I was hoping to get a good-paying job straight out of college. The software industry at that time was going through a major revolution. In 1999, it was scrambling to prepare for a computer problem predicted to occur at the dawn of the new year (Y2K). They needed more talented people to catch the technical problems and come up with a viable solution. Naturally, the demand for software engineers was much higher than their supply, which created a "Golden Gap" opportunity for skilled programmers to benefit from.

I do not know how my father was able to predict the future so accurately. Maybe he picked it up from a book he read, or perhaps he was a visionary! Unequivocally, my father was the reason why I was lucky to have tapped into the zeitgeist when I entered the workforce. As a result of being in the right field at the right time, I had three full-time software engineering job offers in 2000, one year before I graduated college. Two of those offers were from startups that went bust a year later (after 9/11), and one was from a globally recognized brand—Hertz. My hunger for success and growth was at an all-time high. Therefore, I was more inclined to join the startups, but my mother convinced me to go with the internationally established organization. Like all mothers, she wanted the best for her child, and perhaps this advice came from her past experiences.

Hertz is a Florida-based car rental company that started its journey way back in 1918 and was thriving by the time it came to my college for campus placements. It had definitely earned its credibility as an organization by being a part of the big three rental car holding companies in the United States. Hertz hired my cohort of software engineers to build its first-ever e-commerce platform during the early days of digitization in corporate America. This was an era when established brick-and-mortar businesses began realizing that they needed a dot-com address to reach more customers and stay competitive. Companies were actively hiring for software engineering jobs to build their digital platform and create an online presence. Moving a business online during that time was much more complicated and challenging than it is today.

I took up the responsibility to make it happen for Hertz. Initially, the senior management had planned on hiring some fancy consultants to create the e-commerce platform. Let me tell you something serious about these consultants: they even charge you for breathing! Since I had hands-on experience developing software using different programming languages, I was convinced that we could get the job done in-house and save a lot of money in the process. When I started working on this project, I sensed that it was not going to be an easy ride. The timing was of the essence, as it is with all Greenfield market opportunities. My managers were not really confident or happy with the progress me and my team had made until then and were planning to hire a third party to move things fast. Therefore, I decided to put my job on the line to show my commitment toward this goal. I told my boss that if anything went wrong, I would take full responsibility and resign from my position.

With so much at stake, I could not afford to lose again or let my team down. I worked day and night to build a dynamic e-commerce platform that could serve customers from over 200 countries in more than eighteen languages. This journey was a roller-coaster ride, and quite often, I had to make personal sacrifices. There was a time when I did not sleep for forty-eight hours to accomplish a mission impossible. When I told my wife about this "mission impossible," she sarcastically said, "You might as well replace Tom Cruise from the movie series." I won't lie, she had started questioning her life choices, but it turned out to be a great learning experience for me. Eventually, my organization was able to generate over $5 billion using this e-commerce portal! I moved up the ladder very quickly as I led initiatives with my team to build the Hertz digital platform.

By the time I turned twenty-eight, I was leading a large global organization. Surely there was no shortage of hard work and bold actions on my part, but what really contributed to my rapid success was that I had managed to tap into the zeitgeist again with this job. Being involved with an iconic global e-commerce brand at the beginning of its digital transformation journey in Y2K played a major role. I was just in the right place at the right time, thanks to the one time in my life when I was a good son and listened to my mother's advice.

I stayed at Hertz for fourteen years, and most of it was as an "intrapreneur." Perhaps this phase lasted much longer than it should have. I was well-settled in life and felt secure in that job until I could not contain my burning desire to be an entrepreneur. I wanted to give my vision a life of its own, and that wouldn't have been possible without switching to the entrepreneur phase. With the gracious support of my wife, I started my own company in 2015 while she continued to work in a stable job, allowing me to take this bold risk. I'm forever grateful to her for backing my decision despite being fully aware of the risks involved.

In the early days of building Techolution, I thought that we would be creating mobile and web applications for big enterprises. Given the level of demand for these services in the market during that period, we saw a big opportunity to build a profitable business. However, after going out in the field and selling to prospective customers, I realized that my original service offering was what we call a "Redfield market." Although the demand for web and mobile applications was increasing by the day, the level of supply was quickly catching up with this growing demand. I was competing against hundreds of established tech consulting companies and high school students who could build apps for $30 an hour. I was now more aware of what cutthroat competition looks like. I started wondering if my decision to quit a comfortable and high-paying full-time job to start my own business was the right thing to do. But now, there was no going back.

After failing fast and having limited runway, I needed to pivot and find the zeitgeist before running out of funds my wife and I had saved up to start the business. I was hell-bent on finding a Greenfield market opportunity where I could make a real difference with my offerings instead of competing on price with thousands of other players. Therefore, I altered the course of Techolution to establish us as a high-tech digital transformation company. We specialized in cloud solutions, and it so happened that big enterprises and startups with deep pockets were looking to adopt the cloud during that period. Our market offering now was very well aligned with what our target customers needed, and the competition in this space was relatively much lower. Over time, our services expanded, and we successfully added AI and the Internet of Things (IoT) to the list. We realized that to stay competitive in this space for the long term, we had to make our innovations hard to replicate. Therefore, we started focusing on developing valuable intellectual property to build a competitive edge in the market.

In the first six years of our journey, we had the privilege of assisting some renowned global brands in digitizing their business and embracing AI and cloud technology. We successfully partnered with industry leaders like Google to help solve critical business problems for our clients using AI. For instance, we helped WAWA, the convenience store chain, reduce their food wastage during the peak of the pandemic using a fully customized, AI-powered inventory management solution. My vision was to establish Techolution as a brand that is known for "Innovation Done Right" and that too at a guaranteed price. To be very honest, doing innovation at a fixed cost was an ambitious goal because there are a lot of unknown variables that could change the course of things while innovating. However, this approach has helped us create more confidence among our clients, as many companies are comfortable with innovating their businesses at a fixed price.

When you do good work, you are bound to get the recognition that you deserve. In 2019, Techolution made it to the prestigious Inc. 500 club of the Fastest-Growing Companies in America! This was just the beginning of our glorious achievements. In 2022, we were named the "Best Cloud Transformation Company of the Year" by *CIOReview* magazine. During the same year, we also earned the title of "Best in Business" for our entire industry sector by the *Inc.* magazine. I am delighted to have found my zeitgeist very fast, but it was far from easy. However, all the hardship that I endured on my journey, from being a kid who wanted to play soccer to entering the Inc. 500 club as an entrepreneur, was worthwhile. I had mastered the art and science of tapping into the zeitgeist over and over again without having to rely on luck!

CHAPTER 4 – KEY TAKEAWAYS

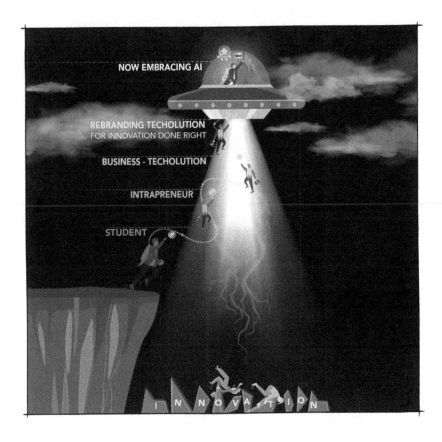

YOUR NOTES

_____

_____

_____

_____

_____

_____

_____

_____

_____

Succeed Faster **SECRET #4**

Turn Fear into Your Superpower

Stop to listen to what your fear is trying to tell you before deciding what actions to take and what actions to avoid. This will help you succeed faster and win often.

CHAPTER 5

TURN YOUR FEAR INTO A SUPERPOWER

T apping into the zeitgeist of your era requires careful evaluation of the underlying circumstances, and your fear can be the best ally in testing the waters before diving into the ocean of your dreams. Contrary to popular belief, fear is not an impediment to success. This is one of the top three mindset changes you will need to make the transition from failing fast to succeeding faster.

We may have been led to believe that fear is the enemy of progress by those who make it look cool to be fearless. I would go so far to say that it is actually ignorant and stupid to try to be fearless! Fear is an inherent gift by nature to help us survive on this planet. It can be our biggest asset once we understand how to leverage it to our advantage. The secret lies in learning how to process our fear for it to work for us.

Successful leaders need to strike a delicate balance between being optimistic dreamers and embracing a healthy dose of realism instilled by their fear that is triggered by the autonomic human nervous system.

The mainstream notion is that you have to be courageous to lead successfully, and fearlessness is a prerequisite for courage. Fear is believed to be the biggest hurdle to accomplishing big things in life, so in principle, the lack of fear should give us what is needed to become successful leaders. However, this is a huge misrepresentation of good leadership!

So, are you fearless? Are you courageous?

There is a very thin line between fearlessness and courageousness. Courage involves taking action despite the presence of fear. It is undoubtedly one of the key traits that is required to be a good leader. Although courage gives us the energy needed to lead the way, it is undeniable that the first movers have a much higher risk of failing than those who follow them. There is an intrinsic risk of failure and pain that comes with leadership. In most cases, this risk causes fear of action that leads to procrastination, which ultimately slows down the pace of growth and evolution on a macro level.

Fear and Evolution

"One small step for man, one giant leap for mankind."

When Neil Armstrong became the first human to step on the moon in 1969, it surely was a giant leap for mankind. Unfortunately, we haven't made many such leaps since that time because fear is slowing down evolution on this planet!

The common belief today is that the world is changing a bit too rapidly and we must slow it down in the best interest of the human race.

Is the world really changing and innovating too fast?

It is true that digital transformation is disrupting life as usual, and innovative startups are displacing big old businesses. But let's rewind the clock and look at the technological evolution we have achieved today versus what society had imagined back in the late 1960s, over six decades ago. We will explore this through the lens of Hollywood science fiction and computer-generated imagery (CGI).

In the late 1960s, there began a television series that would ultimately grow into a cinematic powerhouse: *Star Trek*. From the very first episode in 1966 till many years later, the original *Star Trek* TV series let us imagine what it would be like to travel at light speed across space. It presented a vision of the future where humanity has united and ventured out into space, exploring the vastness of the galaxy aboard starships. From warp drive to transporters and tricoders, the technological prowess demonstrated in this series was way too futuristic. This television show spawned a franchise that survives to this day. But by contrast, where are we with our space technologies? Yes, we've had some limited success with missions to Mars and commercial near-space travel. However, we have yet to experience travel beyond the red planet, let alone intergalactic expeditions. Just imagine where we would be by now if we could transport matter from one place to another and travel across the universe like they did in *Star Trek*!

Some might say that a series like *Star Trek* pushed things too far, so let's look at other advances envisioned by fiction writers and TV series creators to see if that's true. In the popular 1980s TV series called *Knight Rider*, the main character Michael Knight (played by David Hasselhoff) summons his AI-guided self-driving car (KITT), by communicating with a special wristwatch called Comlink. This car actually helps Knight pursue or escape from the bad guys in action scenes because it's equipped with features like super pursuit mode, voice synthesis, and molecular bonded shell. The combination of Michael Knight's skills and KITT's advanced technology makes them a formidable team in fighting crime and assisting those in need. This series gained a cult following and has been praised for its blend of action, adventure, and science fiction elements.

On the big screen, we've seen countless movies where hovercrafts transport people, characters interact in a digital realm through holographic screens, the world is solar-powered and carbon-free, and chronic diseases are a thing of the past.

A quick pulse-check on what we have achieved today is far from the wildest dreams: no one has reached light speed; self-driving emission-free cars are not the new normal; there are still no safe flying cars; we don't live in a carbon-free, solar-powered world; and as I write this book, we have still not fully recovered from the pandemic caused by the novel coronavirus.

We now live in a world where technology, instead of serving us, seems to be turning us into slaves of our own inventions. For instance, most of us look down all day long and live with our attention trapped by whatever is on our mobile screens. In fact, I would submit to you that we have regressed a bit from our expectations of where human civilization would be by now. The survival instinct has taken an unprecedented priority in the past two decades, and I believe this is why our world has become more divisive than ever.

Whenever humanity has to worry about survival, we become divisive and negative. When evolution is the priority, we become more united and optimistic.

We are wired as humans to prioritize survival over evolution and success. It is embedded in us to think about the pain and repercussions of falling hard before we jump higher and venture into uncharted territories. As a result, aiming low, failing fast, and setting the expectation to fail small have become a comfortable and trendy approach for today's leaders.

The fail-fast mindset made a lot of sense in the era when it emerged as a response to a very unstable and volatile world. It was developed as a defensive reaction to a series of big failures that the global economy experienced in the first decade of the new millennia. It all started with the monumental dot-com bubble burst of 2000 and immediately followed by an even bigger catastrophe, the great global financial crisis of 2008! This unfortunate series of economic downturns guaranteed the permanent adoption of the fail-fast mindset in the business world. It was a preemptive coping mechanism for all the pain from the consecutive and colossal failures of that era.

The fail-fast approach addressed some key problems present in its predecessor method, the waterfall project management. However, it virtually erased critical long-term strategic planning and market tests at the ideation stage before entering the costly execution phase.

While failing fast sounds like a safe strategy to many leaders, it is an approach that stifles major innovation and evolution. For the world to evolve faster toward an optimistic vision of the future, we will need many more leaders to be armed with the ability to listen to their fear and transform it into a superpower. In order to achieve this, we should first understand the rules of fear and then leverage it to our advantage!

The Five Rules of Fear

When you are well-versed with the rules of a game, you will be able to play it much better than those who don't know anything about it. Imagine playing baseball without knowing which particular shot will get you a home run. It will be nearly impossible to win against your opponent. Dealing with fear might be the toughest game that you will ever play. However, learning some key rules will definitely give you an upper hand when it comes to turning fear into your superpower.

Rule #1: Being fearless is dumb and ineffective. While fearlessness may seem admirable on the surface, it implies a lack of caution or consideration for potential risks and consequences.

Rule #2: To gain the courage needed to lead the way, fear should neither be suppressed nor overpowered. It is crucial to find the right balance if you want to turn your fear into a source of strength.

Rule #3: **One of the most powerful secrets to success is to always pause to listen to your fear (inner voice) and process what it is trying to tell you before going into action mode.**

Rule #4: Even though a few people are born natural leaders, everyone has the ability to evoke their inner greatness to become successful leaders if and when needed by learning to manage their fears.

Rule #5: Fear is your friend, but procrastinating over the fear of failing is also not going to get you anywhere.

Are you procrastinating because of your fear of failure?

Good leaders cannot afford to procrastinate because to achieve great things in life, you have to perform a massive amount of actions within a specified time frame.

So the next natural question is how do we get rid of fear to avoid procrastination?

To be honest, fearlessness is not a characteristic we should want to see in our leaders because it leads to foolish and rushed actions that increase the odds of failure. You should focus on learning how to process your fear if you want to lead by example. The practice of processing your fears will give you valuable insights and lead you to a well-thought-out plan that can help you avoid the roadblocks, traps, and dead ends, which usually show up on the way to success.

How to Process Your Fear

Listening to your fear and processing it before executing on your ideas will help you succeed faster, but you must remember that fear isn't fact! It is a message from your built-in survival mechanism to alert you of a potential danger ahead. This message can be right quite often, but it can also be wrong sometimes. The feeling of fear is mostly felt in our heart, but it actually stems from a strong and persistent pessimistic thought that pops in our subconscious mind before we take on a new, big, and bold step.

These thoughts usually come in the form of questions that sound like the following:

"What if I F it up?"

"What if I lose what I have and value?"

"What if I harm my health?"

"What if I lose my life?"

These "What if" questions in your head tend to drain your energy thinking about what would happen if you failed while trying.

So should you suppress those negative, sometimes borderline paranoid thoughts?

Well, these thoughts are a part of the human defensive system that is better known as the "inner voice." This is not necessarily a bad voice, but it is also not always the right one! Your subconscious mind tries to bring the inner voice to your attention through the emotion of fear in your heart. As a result, your heart beats faster when you are afraid.

Everything that this voice signals to you may or may not be accurate, but it is surely information coming from your subconscious system based on historical experiences. It could be related to your personal past encounters, something you subconsciously saw or heard. At times, it could even be an important lesson learned by one of your ancestors that has been stored and passed down through your DNA. Some people speculate that the bacteria in your guts are communicating with you since they know a thing or two more about survival than we do. They have survived on this planet way longer than we have, that is, millions of years.

Either way, think of your fear like a close adviser whose job is to play devil's advocate. It doesn't mean it is right or wrong; you just need to stop and evaluate for yourself the credibility of what it's trying to tell you. You must try to understand the message that the thoughts associated with your fear are trying to communicate. This journey of looking deep within yourself will help you realize that the feelings tied to your fear aren't random.

Acknowledging and processing your fear is the easy part. It will start coming to you naturally with some introspection and practice. However, evaluating the accuracy of the fear can be very tricky. It requires a systematic and methodical approach that can also guide you on how to turn your fear into a superpower.

Ten Steps to Turn Your Fear into a Superpower

We clearly have very good reasons to be fearful of taking risky actions. However, instead of inaction and procrastination, let's focus on learning a methodical approach that will empower you to decipher the messages hidden within your fear. This step-by-step guide aims to unlock the potential within that fearful energy so that you can harness it as a source of strength to propel your ideas toward resounding success and unwavering consistency.

STEP 1

Practice on becoming aware the moment you feel fear in your heart.

Imagine yourself standing at the edge of a high diving board, ready to take a leap into the deep pool below. As you prepare to jump, you will feel a flutter of fear in your heart. It's that moment when your mind starts developing different scenarios and questioning the consequences. You are well aware of your fear at this point. Nurturing this awareness is the first step toward turning your fear into a superpower.

STEP 2

The next step is to pause all thoughts and actions for a moment to transition your focus from the physical feeling of fear in the heart to identifying the underlying "What if" questions that are triggering this emotion.

STEP 3

Now, start acknowledging your inner voice by writing down on paper or typing up on the phone the "what if" questions that are in your subconscious. Write all of them down, one by one.

STEP 4

Once you have noted down the underlying "what if" questions, it's time to figure out what you are afraid of losing by taking the action you have in mind. It could be the loss of life, wealth, social status, or reputation. Whatever you are afraid of losing, take a note.

STEP 5

The next step requires pausing to process the potential obstacles and risks in the form of the "what if" questions that you have noted in step 4, one by one.

STEP 6

Now, it is time to assess the reality and severity of each individual risk. Then, score the severity of every "what if" question you wrote down on a scale of 0–10, and do the same for the likelihood of each "what if" risk materializing.

STEP 7

For each one of the risks that score above 6 in likelihood and severity, you need to come up with a plan of action to mitigate them.

Here is an easy-to-follow method to come up with a plan of action:

For each "What if I F this up" question that you noted down, answer the following question:

"How do I not F this up?"

Through this process, you are transforming your problem-oriented inner voice into a solution-driven mindset.

Now, instead of letting "What if I F this up?" hold you back, you begin to focus on "How do I not F this up?"

The key here is every time you have a "What if?" thought that pop into your head, transition it to "How do I?" questions related to the same topic that triggered the fear.

For example, turn "What if my idea fails?" into "How do I know for sure that my idea is aligned with the current growing market needs?"

Keep on drilling down and asking more and more "How do I" questions. This process will lead you to a very detailed and well-thought-out plan that addresses all the risks that your fear helped you identify. It will also give you a powerful confidence deeply supported by intellectual honesty to build and execute your new, low-risk strategy.

STEP 8

Be open-minded to let the fear be right sometimes!

You will often come across fears that are too real and big to overcome. In this scenario, your "what if" questions do not have viable "how do I" answers. In such situations, you have to seriously consider giving up on executing your specific plan and leave space for something more viable to show up. Success isn't only about the actions you take. That's the visible part everyone can see. The invisible secret to success lies in all the actions you thought about taking but didn't pursue because your fear or inner voice made you stop, and instead, you passed on it and did nothing.

STEP 9

Acknowledge and process your team and stakeholders' fears as well.

Good leaders must be always disciplined to brainstorm with their team members to tap into their collective intuitive power. This will magnify your ability to identify the risks of failure and build a plan to mitigate those threats prior to starting your journey. Working with your team to listen to their fears and processing them as a group also ensure longevity of the team spirit. Such groups tend to stick together to work through the toughest moments.

STEP 10

Revisit the previously processed fears as your situations change.

The world is constantly evolving, which forces market conditions to change, and so does the risk. We must iteratively listen to our fears, the collective perception of our team, and external expert opinions even after we have begun executing. This will empower us to proactively identify new risks that emerge and build a plan of action to address them along the journey. It can be done on a daily, weekly, or monthly basis, depending on the volatility of your market and personal life.

We must research and consult with experts who have traveled similar paths before embarking on a new journey. It is a very smart approach to tap into other experts' fears and learn from their mistakes so that we can avoid them in our lives. However, no two journeys are identical, and even an expert's perspective is just one data point, an external outlook that may or may not be applicable to our circumstances. Therefore, we must be rational to consider all the risks and potential roadblocks from both personal and external viewpoints before making a decision. Be careful to only consult experts who have "successfully" ventured on comparable journeys in the past.

Leveraging fear as an intelligence-gathering mechanism and processing it logically on a point-by-point basis is a very easy concept but requires discipline to apply it consistently whenever you are afraid about doing something. Those who master this process will have learned how to listen to their inner voice and develop a very accurate "gut" feeling. It is what we call being intuitive. This simple method will help you boost your confidence by taking a more educated and calculated approach to building your dream.

Following this step-by-step process can help even the most risk-averse people easily process their fear and turn it into a source of strength, which can also be their superpower. However, those who are naturally fearless require a different approach to make the most of their fear deficiency.

Always Pause to Listen to Your Fears

Solution for Fear-Deficient People

On one side, you have plenty of people who experience paralyzing fear that involuntarily shows up whenever they are about to take a risk. The voice simply asks "What if" questions that are discouraging and lead to procrastination.

On the flip side, there is a tiny segment of the population that is naturally fearless. They are born with an overly optimistic inner voice that tells them to "just do it" every time they are about to take a major risky action. The "overly optimistic and overconfident" problem can worsen if their inner circle (friends and family) strongly believes in them and offers no real insights on whether the idea will have merit in the market at the time it will be released.

If you are an overly optimistic person, instead of surrounding yourself only with "yes people," make sure to include enough cautiously pessimistic "what if people" at the ideation and planning stage.

They will help you poke holes in your idea and induce some fear of failing. This is very healthy at the ideation stage to help address important risks of failure before you embark on the journey of building your dream. You will get to make adjustments at the early planning stage before investing any time, money, and resources on execution. It also forces you to get more aware about your market and build expertise by conducting in-depth research of your target segment. This keeps you laser focused on your prospects and creates the momentum needed to achieve the escape velocity to turn your ambitious project into a reality that will go viral and stick for the long term.

For those who struggle with a lack of fear or find themselves frequently labeled as fearless, it is crucial to recognize that embracing fear is not a weakness but a pathway to growth and self-awareness. Keeping a check on our fearlessness is vital to move in the right direction. It can help us succeed faster at innovating toward a world where advanced technologies are available to enrich the human experience so that we can live happier, healthier, and more meaningful lives on this planet and beyond.

◦ Process Your Fear Worksheet ◦

Turn fear into your superpower

A. Clearly describe your fear related to your dream/goal

(for example: My dream/goal is to learn skydiving, but I'm afraid of falling to the ground from a high altitude)

C. Find out why these "What If" questions have been triggered
(For example : You might have seen some parachute failures on TV)

1.

2.

3.

D. Use Stats and Logical Reasoning to score the Likelihood and Severity of each "What If" risk materializing
(For example : Likelihood of parachutes not opening is 0.1% time; Parachutes not opening can lead to death so severity is high)

What if Risk(s)	Likelihood of Occurrence (Out of 100%)	Severity of impact (Out of 10; highest value = 10)

(for example : What if my parachute fails to open)

1.

2.

3.

E. For risks having either a high severity (above 6) or likelihood score (above 60%), create a Plan of Action by asking "How Do I" questions
(For example : **How Do I** ensure that my parachute doesn't malfunction while skydiving? By choosing reputed Skydiving instructors)

What if Risk(s) (Problem Oriented)	How Do I (Solution Oriented)	Plan of Action (Practical Solution)

{ fear done right }

103

CHAPTER 5 – KEY TAKEAWAYS

YOUR NOTES

_____

_____

_____

_____

_____

_____

_____

_____

_____

_____

_____

Succeed Faster **SECRET #5**

Work Smart before Working Hard

because hard work alone does not pay off. Learning how to work smart before working hard is the most effective principle to succeed faster.

CHAPTER 6

WORKING HARD DOES NOT PAY OFF

L earning to channel our fearful energy into a source of strength can surely eliminate procrastination and give us the ability to work hard. However, working hard will only get you so far in life because you will be trading your hours for dollars when you simply focus on the "hard" part. Very soon, you will reach the upper limit on how much you can succeed because there are only twenty-four hours in a day. That is why you need to learn how to work smart first to get to the next level of success and achieve your big goals.

It took me almost forty years to realize this, and I learnt only after having worked a little too hard to achieve the first major milestone of my grandiose dream.

I was born an introvert, but while growing up, I learnt how to become an extrovert when needed to achieve my leadership goals and entrepreneurial dreams. Generally speaking, I like to remain private about my achievements because of my introverted nature. However, when it comes to business, I strongly believe in promoting my victories as long as it provides the branding and exposure I need to grow faster.

In 2019, my brainchild Techolution made it to the Inc. 500 club of Fastest-Growing Companies in America! I flew to Phoenix to collect this prestigious award on behalf of the company that I started in 2015 and had been leading for four years at that point. This was the first major win that I achieved, and it was very public in nature. I did not try to hide it from my social circle because of the impact the publicity would have on my company's market credibility.

I remember being really annoyed when a family member called to say, "Congratulations, Luv, hard work always pays off in the end. I am proud of you."

In my head, I was thinking: "That is total BS!." I really wanted to correct them. Indeed I worked very hard to accomplish this major milestone, but this was nothing new. I had always worked hard before, and I knew in my bones that it was not the main ingredient for the landmark feat that I achieved in 2019.

Don't get me wrong. I so wished that reaching major milestones in life was as easy as just putting in the hard work. Almost everybody can work hard if they really want to.

Thankfully, my better judgment kicked in on time, and I realized that starting an argument with a well-wishing family member would be futile. I courteously responded with a simple "Thank you, I really appreciate you calling to congratulate me."

This interaction led me to introspect my personal beliefs about success. While growing up, I learned a lot of important guiding principles from my father, and I really respect him for all the great things he taught me in the brief seventeen years that I got to spend with him before he passed. There is one principle that stuck with me and defined the first decade and a half of my career: "Hard work always pays off in the end."

I am sure this is a commonly held belief in society, and most of us grew up learning some flavor of it. Another popular version of this principle that I heard often while growing up was, "No pain, no gain." It sounded cool back then. However, reflecting on it now, I wonder how messed up such a world must be, where the only way to gain something positive is by experiencing a lot of pain and sacrifices.

I strongly lived by this principle for the first sixteen years of my career until it became clear through experience that it's a very flawed and inaccurate perspective of the real world.

It hit me at this point that it was time to unlearn the popular "hard work always pays off in the end" belief if I wanted to accelerate my journey toward super success.

Looking at society from a broader perspective, you will find that some of the hardest-working people out there have two or three jobs. They work every hour of the day that they are not sleeping. Many of them may be earning only minimum wage and have to work really hard just to feed their families and provide safe shelter for them. Even though these people put in a lot of hours, they barely make ends meet.

I personally know a lot of people who work so hard but don't feel like they are achieving much success. Most individuals who work long hours regularly do so because they do not know any other way to earn a living. They have no alternative means of surviving and giving themselves and their families the hope of a better future. In spite of being aware of the statistics, if we still tell someone that hard work always pays off, we would be giving them false hope.

Perhaps, the hardworking poor and middle-class people are being brainwashed with this lie so that they can continue serving the elites at lower costs without much upward mobility. In fact, some of the high achievers don't work that hard after achieving a level of success because they can hire other qualified people to help them continue being successful and achieve new milestones. A small percentage of the rich people who work as hard as the poor and middle class do so because they love what they do and may be addicted to working long hours. For some, pulling all-nighters at work is a good way to distract themselves from other problems in their lives.

I know that many of you might be puzzled, and some upset, at my controversial statement: hard work **does not always** pay off in the end. It goes against everything we have been taught so far by society. Before you tear up this chapter and call it "BS," consider that I have lived by this belief for a very long time. It took me over a decade to see with my open eyes that the reality is quite different. In this chapter, we will look at an alternative strategy that is much more effective at getting you to your goal faster and is a lot less painful than simply working hard. Before we dive into the alternative strategy, I want to share an interesting story from the days when I blindly believed that hard work always pays off in the end.

The Nonstop Drive

Once upon a time, I decided to embark on a thrilling road trip that spanned from the bustling streets of New York all the way to the vibrant shores of Miami. For those of you who are unfamiliar with this route, the total road distance is over 1,300 miles, and it takes nearly nineteen hours to reach the destination if you drive nonstop. A road trip like this surely sounds fun and adventurous, but when you plan to drive for nineteen hours straight, it can prove to be a regretful decision.

Before we dive deeper into this story, let me tell you that during this phase of my life, I was young and stupid with the mindset of "work hard and play hard." The year was 2005, and I had recently got married at the time. The thought of driving across the sprawling landscapes with my wife was captivating enough to lure me in without a second thought. After doing some basic Internet searches and randomly flipping through travel guides, I quickly made up my mind for this road trip. Back then, I did not own a Tesla FSD because a self-driving car was still a futuristic thing that we could only imagine or experience through sci-fi movies and TV series. However, I did own a yellow Mini Cooper with a black top, and it offered a really smooth driving experience for a car in its segment. Besides my wanderlust, the primary motivation was to save money, as flight ticket prices for this route were relatively high back then, especially on the Presidents' Day long weekend in February.

After hastily planning my trip, I quickly jumped onto the execution phase, all ready to get behind the wheel and start my nonstop drive to the city of Miami. I remember it was a bright sunny New York morning, so I decided to put my shades on. I also created a special playlist because it was going to be a long journey. Since we did not have the luxury of using Spotify in those days, I spent quite

111

some time manually adding songs and testing this driving playlist. The first few hours on the road felt like a nice break from my daily work routine. We were cruising down the road, enjoying the beautiful view, and even singing along to our favorite songs.

After ten hours of continuous driving, my excitement wore down, and I started losing focus on the road. It escalated to the point where I almost hit a truck on the highway because I was distracted. Very soon, I realized that I would have to change the "nonstop" plan if I wanted to reach my destination safely.

Since we barely managed to escape an accident, my wife asked me to get something that would keep me awake and focused for the drive ahead. While we were looking left and right to find a convenience store, I somehow glanced at the fuel indicator. It was almost touching the red line. Now, we had to find a gas station as well. Our search got intense when we were unable to locate one after driving for over ten minutes. The next few miles on the road tested my patience to another level. I was finally able to find a gas station with a stocked-up convenience store. I stopped there for a while to refuel my car and also got coffee for my human engine. After this short pause, I got behind the wheel again, all ready for another ten-hour stint. Unfortunately, it did not last very long this time.

Two hours later, when the caffeine had lost its grip on my mind, the exhaustion seeped in and derailed my progress. I quickly dozed off and woke up finding myself on the shoulder lane, almost off-roading into a tree on the sidelines of the highway. Fortunately, there weren't many cars on the road at that time, so we did not get into an accident. This was happening for the second time in a span of two hours. I was really embarrassed, and now I got the top spot on my wife's list of worst drivers in the world. It was about 2:00 a.m., and we were in the middle of nowhere. After looking at some signboards, I got to know that we were somewhere near South Carolina. Still a very long way from Miami, 630 miles to be precise. I had to accept the fact that there was no way we could make it to our destination safely without stopping for the night.

We started searching for hotels to get some rest so that I could start my drive in the morning without any hiccups. The part of South Carolina where I almost crashed my car was very sparsely populated, so I pulled over to the next town in search of a decent hotel. But surely, all we found was a dingy motel, and they wanted to charge us $200 for one night in cash since they knew we had no other choice. That is a lot of money for a shady motel, even by today's standards. At that time, $200 was a lot of money for me. I was left with no choice but to spend all the cash I had for the room, only to find mold on the bed sheets after I made the payment. We had a fair share of trouble that night, so we ended up sleeping on the room's floor to keep ourselves safe from mold infections. My wife was furious, and I don't blame her because we were recently married, and this was our first long drive after the marriage. I should have planned better.

Laying on that gloomy motel room's floor, with my clothes and boots on, sent me into a flashback. When I was planning this trip, I thought that I was going to save a lot of time and money, which would allow us to enjoy a pleasant vacation in Miami. However, this journey ended up taking me twenty-seven hours instead of nineteen and cost me $200 more than I had planned. Not to forget that I almost crashed my car, which could have further added to my expenses. I was upset then, and I am still upset today about wasting $200 on a dirty motel room, only because I thought working hard would be rewarding.

If I had the wisdom to prioritize smart work, I would have researched and prepared more for this trip. I would have known that it's not feasible to drive for nineteen hours straight. Instead of a shady motel room, we might have experienced the hospitality of a branded hotel with a clean bed and a nice dinner for less than half of what I actually spent. When you add the cost of a hotel and food for an overnight stop for two people, flying would have definitely been cheaper and way faster. This was the first time I realized that working hard does not guarantee the desired outcomes.

My Epiphany

"Hard work always pays off in the end."

This age-old principle was ingrained in me from a very young age by my dear father who wished nothing but the best for me. He was a pharmacist by profession who always worked hard to provide the best for his family, and his strong work ethics became a great source of inspiration for me. Therefore, I never questioned this principle for a very long time until it became a major hurdle in the path of my exponential growth.

In the early stages of my professional journey, my belief in this age-old principle grew stronger as it helped me achieve a relatively high amount of success. I started my working career at the age of twenty-one as a software engineer with a reputed global organization called Hertz. Since I had always believed that working hard will get me the desired results, I adopted that approach here as well. My unwavering commitment to accomplishing even seemingly impossible goals helped me achieve a relatively high amount of success very early. By the age of twenty-six, I was the global director of a very large and important business unit for a Fortune 500 company with over 30,000 employees.

Many of you might say that "your hard work really paid off," so why should we not follow the same approach to achieve our goals? Well, because in hindsight, even though I was always working hard and accomplished more significant goals than my peers, I did not necessarily achieve more success and recognition than them. I was the guy who was always taking one for the team. Most of the time, I used to start my workday at 7:00 a.m. and would stay in the office till 11:00 p.m. I became habitual of working sixteen to twenty hours daily, including the weekend, for no extra pay. Since I loved what I used to do and was always looking for new missions to accomplish, it did not feel like a burden for me.

What about work-life balance? Well, I will just say that my wife was not particularly happy with my "hard work" and long office hours because my job officially required me to work only from Monday to Friday, that too between 8:15 a.m. and 4:30 p.m. There were times when I did not sleep for twenty-four to forty-eight hours straight because I was working on critical projects. I'm not blaming my employer and managers for this, because I chose to work hard and put in those extra hours. In fact, no employer can make anyone work the kind of hours I did sometimes. This is a personal choice. I spent over a decade working extremely hard, and it didn't necessarily pay off any more than it would have if I had worked just as much as my peers. Time and again, I saw some colleagues getting the same type of promotions as me, even though they worked a lot less than I did. There were some who moved up the corporate ladder faster by working significantly less hard.

When I saw that my hard work was not being appreciated and reciprocated with the level of rewards and recognition that it deserved, I started blaming the corporate environment for being unfair and unjust. Instead of introspecting about what I was missing, I started believing that the big company reward and recognition model was tainted with the typical corporate politics where they favored the politicians over high performers. I won't say that my opinions were based on false premises and did not even have an iota of truth to it. However, the tainted rewards and recognition model was not necessarily the only reason why I was stuck in the same upper-middle management role for over five years.

At that point in my career, I had the choice to drink the Kool-Aid and take it easy by becoming a corporate politician. However, that would not have done justice to the type of person I am. I have always been a dreamer and builder at heart, and working hard to accomplish a challenging task was a part of my DNA. Therefore, I decided to quit my job to reset my career in an environment that was more fair and rewarding. In 2015, I finally set out on the path of entrepreneurship by starting my own company, Techolution.

When you are working at a secure high-paying job, you get accustomed to certain things in life, and compromising on that can feel like a struggle. The first few years were very challenging and filled with hard work with no easy or quick reward. Since I had always excelled in my working career, not seeing the desired results in the early days of my entrepreneurship journey made me question my decision to start a business. Quite often, I would be drowning in anxiety instead of welcoming the weekend on Friday nights. I wondered if my hard work would ever pay off or if my business would fail like 90 percent of the startups do. I had nobody else to blame for this time, so it forced me to learn the reality that hard work alone does not pay off.

Therefore, I propose to all of you that it's time to unlearn all the catchy, old beliefs we grew up with. They may sound motivational to those who feel that they have no other choice. However, these beliefs are simply not true and should be replaced with one that pays off sooner rather than later. For example, "work smart before working hard."

Learn to Work Smart before Working Hard

Humans are creatures of habit. For us, unlearning an old habit takes much more time and effort than learning a new one.

Working hard to succeed in life also transitions into a habit for most people because they follow it on a daily basis.

Unlearning the age-old principle of "hard work always pays off in the end" becomes more challenging because it is deeply rooted in us. However, it is crucial to debunk this myth because only working hard might lead you to destinations that are not the right end for you.

My personal experiences with working hard have taught me that it will not "always" result in fruitful outcomes. Therefore, I was forced to find a new guiding principle that provides an unlimited potential for exponential growth:

Figure out how to work smart before trying to work hard.

Before we unpack this new guiding principle, let's take a look at what exactly does it mean to "work smart."

Working smart requires you to first figure out the minimum skills, processes, and resources that are needed to achieve the maximum amount of progress toward your end goal in the least amount of time possible.

The implied prerequisite to working smart is that you are crystal clear on your end goal. In other words, you need to have a very concise definition of success that is not going to change on a day-to-day basis until you reach your destination.

Working smart is the first step to success. You should consider working hard only after you have learned how to work smart. This will help you accelerate your wins to super success.

The only way to exponentially grow your achievements and income is not by increasing the number of hours you put in but through the amount of value you bring to your market in exchange for credibility and money, a lot of money!

Before you insist on pushing your way toward your goals with hard work, always take out some time to focus on learning the victory formula that works best for you. I strongly believe that smart work formulas do not follow a "one-size-fits-all" approach. What may have worked for someone else in the past may not effectively work for you in this time frame.

Regardless of the problem you are trying to solve for your market, the profession you want to become an expert at, or the innovation you are aiming to break through, first take the time to explore how it actually works. Research and learn to find the best strategy to achieve your end goal with minimum effort and resources before working too hard trying to accelerate toward your destination.

Another way to look at the relationship between success, smart work, and hard work is:

Working smart is about carefully choosing what you will focus your attention on in the long term as well as on a very short-term basis.

The smart work approach requires you to develop the skill of being highly effective at focusing your attention only on the one activity that will help you make the biggest leap toward your destination. Learning to figure out when hard work will pay off versus when to slow down to take a rest or build expertise before taking action is also a crucial aspect of working smart.

On the other hand, hard work is a measure of the amount of time you put into working to achieve your set goals.

The more time you invested into working, the harder you would have worked. It does not take into consideration how effective the extra effort is in helping you achieve your goal.

Let's say that I am driving a car from point A to B by taking a route that requires ten hours. Alternatively, there is a path that can get me to point B in just six hours, but I am not aware of it because of my limited research. In this case, driving four extra hours does not add any value, even though it is hard work because it will get me to the same destination. I would have saved myself some time and effort had I known about the second route prior to starting my journey.

The Seven Rules for Working Smart

Hard work is essential but not sufficient to help you move faster toward your destination. Working hard at doing more "smart work" as quickly as possible is the key to achieving super success, regardless of where you start and what goal you want to accomplish. Here are some thumb rules for working smart that can help you avoid the pain of doing mindless hard work from the very beginning of your journey.

Rule #1: Avoid brute forcing your way to success by just increasing the number of hours you put into your efforts.

Rule #2: Master the core skills needed to bring real value to your market because the more value you add, the more successful you will be.

Rule #3: Build a highly productive team that believes in your vision and is committed to accomplishing the mission because "If you want to go fast, go alone. If you want to go far, go together."

Rule #4: Start working harder only when you have found a clear path to your destination and have achieved a level of mastery to get you there faster.

Rule #5: Learn to figure out when slowing down is better than working harder to avoid burning out. Take the time needed to focus on rebuilding your energy and attention to find the most effective way forward toward your next destination.

Rule #6: Slow down growth, if needed, to improve your processes, and make your execution highly effective and scalable at the beginning of every new growth phase along your journey.

Rule #7: Develop automation and innovative intellectual property to accelerate growth and profits for your business.

Learn and Practice the Winning Moves before Executing

Learning the rules of working smart is a nonnegotiable for achieving the next level of success in life. Once you are well-versed with these rules, you have to apply them to figure out the winning moves before actually going into execution mode.

There are two ways to learn and master the winning moves. The first one requires learning from your own mistakes, which comes under the purview of hard work. In this case, you might waste a lot of time and effort figuring out what works and what doesn't. However, the second method follows the smart work principle. It can help you learn what to do and what to avoid from other successful people's journeys rather than figuring out the winning moves on your own by failing repeatedly before eventually succeeding at some point.

It is highly recommended to adopt the second guiding principle if you want to move faster toward your ultimate destination, but there is a catch. You cannot just blindly follow someone's failures and wins to build your own path to success. It requires a meticulous analysis of their winning moves, the underlying circumstances, the time period, and a lot more.

You can choose to learn how to work smart from successful mentors by reading their books, researching their content online, or taking a course. However, it is of utmost importance to find a worthy mentor with the trophies and battle scars who can take you under their wings and teach you what they know. Whatever you are trying to achieve, only learn from an expert who knows how to do it already and has evidence to support their claims.

Once you find your winning formula by learning from a true master in the field, you have to test it and mold it into a version that works effectively for you.

Before my epiphany, I firmly believed that "hard work always pays off in the end." I can recall quite a few times when I tried to succeed at something with brute force powered by my hard work, only to fail over and over again. It took me about five years to actually become a master at "working smart before working hard" since I first realized that there was a better and faster way to succeed in life.

For example, before starting my business in 2015, I thought I could rely on my grit and expertise in building and leading teams to develop great software solutions for clients. Admittedly, I did not research deeply enough with reputed entrepreneurs in my industry as to what it would take to build a successful business from scratch. If I had known that the odds of succeeding were so low, let's be honest, I might not have quit my job.

Before starting my own business, I had a secure high-paying job, a stable family with kids, and a nice home. Life was great, and starting a business would not be worth the trouble had I known the real risk. Of course, great was not enough for me, and I wanted a lot more for my life. So I went out on my own to prepare myself for the giant leap from great to greatest.

I quickly discovered that execution and delivery is not the first step in building a business. The very first thing you need to do is to convince a total stranger that they need what your business has to offer. This stranger should fit in the category of your prospective customers. The point I am trying to make here is that you have to be able to get others to pay for your product or service. In simple words, you have to be really good at sales.

Albeit late, this was the moment when I realized that real entrepreneurship wasn't exactly what they show you on reality TV. What works in real life is not what you learn from your favorite investors on *Shark Tank*. This is also when it hit me that everybody's least favorite shark, Kevin O'Leary, a.k.a. "Mr. Wonderful," was right all along when he said:

"Cash flow is the lifeline of every business. Sales is the only way to generate cash flow for a startup because no bank will lend you money on day 1 and no investor will fund an unproven startup with a founder who has no track record of building successful businesses."

I knew all about technology, but I was starting from square one when it came to sales and business. I assumed that selling would be easy and anyone could do it as long as they had a good product or service to offer and knew who their target customers were. However, it was proving to be very difficult as I was bombing all the meetings that I managed to land with clients during the early days of my entrepreneurship journey. I realized that I should stop working harder to land more meetings and pitch my company's services to prospective clients because it was simply not working. I needed to learn the winning moves first, which, in this case, translated to learning sales.

I was left with two options: I could either hire an expert salesperson in my industry or develop my sales skills as quickly as possible before running out of money and being forced to go find another corporate job. I chose the latter and went to acquire the sales skills on my own because I could not afford to hire a seasoned sales executive at that point. I started reading all the books I could find from reputable sales gurus and followed their content on YouTube. I also reached out to some of the most seasoned salespeople who sold to me when I was their client. They used to wine and dine me, and now I was buying them nice meals in exchange for their valuable advice that would hopefully help me learn the pro techniques quickly enough to generate revenue so that my business could survive another quarter. See how the tables have turned now.

Week by week, I was learning more and practicing the latest sales concepts on new potential clients. Within the first three months, I was able to close my first deal. That feeling of closing my very first deal is hard to express in words. In the next few months, I was selling like a pro while overseeing my business's operations full-time. I kept on closing every other deal that came my way to the point where selling became fun, and I was hooked to it like anything. In the very first year of starting my business, I sold services that had an accumulated value of over $250K. In the next year, I broke well past the $1M ceiling. By the third year, I was doing $6M of sales on my own, without a business development team! My company grew exponentially for four straight years until I felt that the next smartest move would be to slow down the growth and invest time in developing a sales team to drive the next growth wave of my business.

If I could go back in time and do it all over again, I would have spent more time researching, planning, and learning the art of selling before quitting my job and announcing to the world that I was starting the next cool technology business. I would have been more diligent and proactive toward finding my "Mr. Miyagi" and practiced the "wax on, wax off" until I was equipped with the essential sales skills required to go to the ruthless battlefield of entrepreneurship.

Wax On, Wax Off—Master Your Winning Moves

The "wax on, wax off" concept gained widespread recognition through its portrayal in a movie titled *The Karate Kid*. In this iconic film, the determined teenager Daniel LaRusso, portrayed by actor Ralph Macchio, approaches Mr. Miyagi, a wise and enigmatic karate master played by actor Pat Morita.

The plot revolves around Daniel, an ordinary kid who faces relentless bullying from a group of aggressive karate students. He seeks Mr. Miyagi's guidance to learn karate and defend himself from the bullies. Intrigued by his determination, Mr. Miyagi reluctantly agrees to mentor him. However, instead of teaching Daniel karate moves immediately, he takes an unconventional approach.

Daniel finds himself immersed in a series of seemingly mundane tasks assigned by his new mentor. From waxing his mentor's vintage car to painting the fences, Daniel dutifully carries out each chore with unwavering commitment. As he tirelessly performs the "wax on, wax off" motion, his frustration grows. Yet, his persistence pushes him to seek answers. Little does he know that these repetitive movements hold a deeper purpose. Gradually, he begins to realize that these seemingly unrelated tasks are actually building his muscle memory and honing his reflexes for karate. The repetitive motions serve as a foundation for his training, secretly transforming him into a formidable martial artist.

Fueled by newfound determination, Daniel intensifies his practice and spends countless hours refining his technique. Along this journey, the mentor-student bond between Daniel and Mr. Miyagi deepens, with moments of levity and profound life lessons intertwined. The transformative power of Daniel's training becomes evident as he confronts his bullies in the climactic karate champion-ship. With grace and skill, he faces his opponents head-on, proving that discipline and the guidance of a wise mentor can empower one to overcome any obstacle.

The "wax on, wax off" routine serves as a symbol of the trans-formative journey Daniel undertakes as he evolves from a frustrated teenager to a skilled martial artist. Through perseverance, resilience, and the guidance of Mr. Miyagi, Daniel discovers not only the physical prowess of karate but also the inner strength and character that define his true potential.

Similarly, when you are practicing the winning moves that will help you achieve your goals, performing a simple act over and over again will help you build strong foundational blocks. Instead of learning along the way of fighting a battle and then losing it in the end, you should prioritize practicing the right move and mastering it through repetition by listening to your mentor's advice. This will help you once you figure out how to do things the right way.

Caution: Not everybody who sounds and looks like Mr. Miyagi out there is a real one.

Work Smart by Learning from the Right Mentor

Just as the kid sought guidance from the wise Mr. Miyagi to learn the karate moves in the film, aspiring individuals often look forward to a mentor's teachings to accelerate their journey toward their goals. In today's world, the easy accessibility of information on the World Wide Web has led to an increase in the number of self-proclaimed experts. Therefore, it is crucial to navigate the sea of mentors with discretion if you want the right advice.

When you choose to learn from a mentor's experience instead of wasting time and effort on trial and error, you are definitely moving ahead on the path of working smart first. This will help you avoid the mistakes and get you to your destination a lot faster and cheaper than you would have by learning through your personal failures. However, I must caution you that there are many imposter coaches who will trick you into learning how to be successful in your field from them in exchange for money or equity in your startup.

Mentors are great, but having a fake or bad one is worse than having no mentor and figuring it out on your own. There are many fake gurus out there, so be careful!

I have come across quite a few imposter mentors in my career. In hindsight, there were red flags very early on, but I ignored the signs because they were referred to me by people I knew. Many of these con men, posing as mentors and coaches, are swindlers who are only good at talking and telling stories. You should definitely stay away from them. Besides swindlers, if the mentor you are considering is successful in a completely different domain that is not transferable to yours, then they are not qualified to give you any meaningful, practical advice.

Imagine an aspiring plumber picking the best heart surgeon in their neighborhood to teach them how to master plumbing. No matter how intelligent, successful, and well-meaning this heart surgeon may be, there is not much they can teach you about plumbing.

Not all mentors possess the depth of knowledge, experience, and genuine desire to help others succeed in their journey. It is imperative to develop a keen eye if you want to distinguish between those who simply talk the talk and those who have the substance and dedication to walk the walk. So how can you do that? Well, there are some critical rules that you can learn and apply whenever you come across a potential mentor. These rules will help you filter the noise and stay away from fake gurus who claim to have mastered everything worth learning in the universe.

Five Critical Rules for Selecting the Right Mentor

Many of you might find it overwhelming to search for your Mr. Miyagi, and rightly so, given the high number of fake mentors in the market who claim to make you the next Steve Jobs, Bill Gates, or Elon Musk. I faced similar challenges in my journey, and I know how hard it is to find a genuine mentor who has the required expertise and experience to help you succeed. Therefore, I developed a set of guidelines to evaluate the credibility of a potential mentor before seeking any advice from them. The following are the rules that anyone can apply to find the right mentor:

Rule #1: If any mentor you are considering claims to be very successful, but you cannot find out about their achievements and associations online or from highly trusted sources who witnessed their success, then it is best to assume that they are faking it.

Rule #2: If the mentor has been referred to you by someone and has a very limited online presence, and their LinkedIn profile does not directly depict the success they claim to have achieved, then it is safe to assume that they are exaggerating it. I have heard all kinds of stories like "My LinkedIn profile was hacked, so I had to disable it" or "I am too successful to talk about it online, how come you never heard about my achievements before."

Rule #3: If your mentor's accomplishments are not recent (past five to seven years) and are not directly relevant to your industry, then you should take their advice with a grain of salt. Most likely, their lessons will be outdated and not very useful to you in current times. All they may be able to give you is generic business advice, which can be found on the Internet by "gurus" for free, so please do not waste your money on it!

Rule #4: Don't be so desperate to find a good mentor that you ignore all the red flags. If your gut feeling doubts the credibility of a mentor you are considering, you must dig deeper to find the truth. Fake mentors will take your money, waste your time, and teach you things that will set you back instead of giving you a boost. It will take you even longer to unlearn the wrong things that they have taught you.

Rule #5: It is better to have no mentor than to have a bad one. A bad mentor can do a lot of damage, and some of it might even be irreparable at times. Be patient, and keep on searching more till you find the right one.

The five rules mentioned here can be used as a litmus test to find the right mentor who can help you work smart on a daily basis.

Make Working Smart a Daily Habit

As humans, we tend to create habits that make us robotic until we have to react to unplanned events that threaten our status quo. Our survival instinct makes it normal for us to respond differently to critical uncertain circumstances that can impact our lives. Nevertheless, most people are robotic when it comes to their everyday activities. It suits well for jobs that involve repetitive tasks, like those found in manufacturing and traditional office environments. But with rapid advancements in automation reshaping the employment landscape, machines will soon take over these repetitive jobs.

I am not against sticking to routines and creating daily habits. However, achieving a major dream in today's fast-paced world requires evolution and innovation at the core, which demands smart work. Therefore, we need to make it a part of our daily habits. We cannot catch up with an ever-evolving world without adopting the principle of working smart first.

In modern times, smart work is not a mere choice but a necessity. It requires us to re-evaluate our approach to productivity, embrace flexibility, improve efficiency, and continuously seek opportunities to learn and grow.

Knowing when to stay focused and be repetitive, when to innovate and evolve, and when to react to social noise is the daily discipline of working smart.

It is about finding the right balance between sticking to what works, exploring new possibilities, and filtering out unnecessary distractions. The modern age is filled with constant noise and dopamine boosters, thanks to the Internet and mobile devices. Reacting to every notification will render us totally paralyzed and lost.

By developing the daily habit of working smart, you can maximize your productivity and achieve long-term success. But first, you need to learn the steps that must be followed to work smart every day.

Nine Steps to Work Smart Every Day

Working smart did not come naturally to me in the early stages of my professional career. I relied on "hard work" to achieve any goal for several years until I was forced to find a different approach. My quest to find a better guiding principle to accomplish new milestones faster led me on the path of an exciting discovery. It helped me figure out how to work smart. I have created a step-by-step guide that can be followed by anyone who wants to succeed faster by working smart every day:

1. At the very start of your work day, stop all consumption of new information, and do not take any action. Sit in silence without any distractions for a while.

2. Take ten to fifteen minutes to introspect, and fill out the daily success sheet provided on the next page.

3. Reflect on how well you did yesterday. Think about your major wins, and celebrate them.

4. Evaluate what prevented you from mastering your craft/skills yesterday and what you can do to become the best version of yourself today.

5. Write down your definition of long-term success. It will remind you clearly of your end goal and put you in the right frame of mind to make smart choices on the next step. This is also known as your vision statement. We will learn more about how to set a strong long-term vision in chapter 8.

6. Define up to three important things you need to accomplish today that will help you make the leap toward your destination. Let's call them your "Wow Factor" for the day! Go above and beyond to deliver the highest quality of work on your wow factor.

7. Now, clearly describe up to five "Deal Breaker" tasks that you must perform today for the survival of your business and prevent it from falling behind. Do not pick the things that are not critical on that particular day, and do not go above and beyond when working on these tasks. Doing the bare minimum on your Deal Breakers and going above and beyond on your carefully selected wow factor is the key to working smart on a day-to-day basis.

8. Refer to this daily success sheet as and when needed to check whether you are making progress toward your destination. Stay focused on your predefined goals for the day, and only make adjustments in case of emergencies.

9. The practice of filling out the daily success sheet (provided on the next page) at the beginning of your workday will help you develop the habit of working smart without fail. Be very thoughtful when selecting your key wow factors that matters the most today. Repeat this process regularly to improve your odds of success.

This step-by-step process has been meticulously curated to help you develop a mindset and an approach that prioritizes efficiency and effectiveness over mere busyness. From mastering time management and prioritization to fostering a growth-oriented mindset, these steps will help you optimize your workflow and achieve exceptional results.

• Daily Success Plan •

Work smarter before working harder everyday

Date :

Time :

A.   Mastery of Craft Yesterday

(0 - 10) ____

B. Key Wins Yesterday

1. ____
2. ____
3. ____

C. Personal Action to Improve Your Mastery of Craft Today.

D. Your Vision (Crystal Clear Definition of your long term Success at the end goal)

____
____
____

"Improve your game by just 1% daily over the previous day and you will be twice as good in 70 days"

Key Goals for Today.   - Prioritize what MUST be done to make today super productive!

E. WOW Factors - Leap towards your vision.

☐ 1. ____
☐ 2. ____
☐ 3. ____

F. Deal Breakers - Avoid major setbacks on the path to your vision.

☐ 1. ____   ☐ 4. ____
☐ 2. ____   ☐ 5. ____
☐ 3. ____

{ today done right }

CHAPTER 6 – KEY TAKEAWAYS

YOUR NOTES

_____

_____

_____

_____

_____

_____

_____

_____

_____

_____

_____

CHAPTER 7

THE ZEITGEIST—A MARKET TIMING DEEP DIVE

"Work smart before working hard" is a principle that you can adopt to find your zeitgeist faster, which will help you expedite your journey to success. As discussed in chapter 3, where we introduced the zeitgeist, market timing is the most important factor that determines whether your idea will be successful, super successful, or a painful failure. To succeed fast and consistently, you must commit to being extremely disciplined at pursuing the costly execution phase only after you have confirmed that your business idea follows one of the two winning market timing strategies.

To transform an idea into a super-successful business, you have to become a champion at tapping into the zeitgeist before your funding and the market's attention span for your solution expires.

There is a whole spectrum of achievements between survival and success. Not to forget that several factors need to come together to build a successful company, such as team skills, attitude, motivation, funding, and the quality of execution. However, there's something critical that must be done before you even take the first step toward building your dream. You have to validate how well your idea is aligned with the spirit and mood of the era, that is, the zeitgeist.

In this chapter, we will explore how to methodically calculate the probability of your idea tapping into the zeitgeist. We will also deep dive into the four market timing strategies and the effectiveness of each one of them. At the end of this chapter, we will introduce you to some highly valuable tools like the Zeitgeist Predictive Model that reveal how closely your business idea aligns with the powerful market forces, offering insight into your likelihood of success. However, to leverage the full potential of these tools, you must understand the fundamental economic concepts that play a crucial role in shaping different market timing conditions.

Economics 101—The Foundation of the Zeitgeist

After decades of research, reflection, and analysis, I have found that the most reliable guiding principle that all business and investment decisions can safely rely upon is a fundamental concept taught in Economics 101.

The secret to finding perfect market conditions is hidden in the study of supply and demand trends over time and in identifying the right timing, which fits one of the two winning strategies that are great opportunities for new product/service introductions.

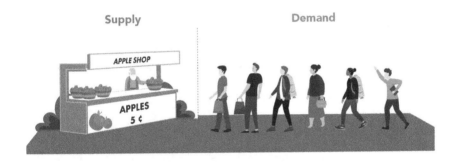

There are many external factors that can significantly affect the supply-demand relationship of a product over time. For example, an unplanned event, such as a pandemic, can lead to a sudden increase in demand for masks and protective equipment. Due to the time it takes to recognize the surge in demand and the confidence that it will last, new competitors can take anywhere from weeks to years to supply the additional quantity of masks needed to fulfill the growing requirements. During this period, when the supply catches up with demand, the early movers with a reliable product may benefit tremendously by selling their offerings at a higher price.

The more complex it is to create a new supply after the demand is validated, the longer an early mover can benefit from the difficulty faced by new competitors to enter the market. However, if the established players or early movers take advantage of their monopoly to charge exorbitant pricing or provide terrible customer service, their consumers will flock to the competition the moment competitive supply floods the market.

Savvy early movers like Amazon and Google invest in creating great user experiences, charging a fair price, and innovating further for their target audience, which leads to long-lasting customer loyalty. This is the best and most sustainable way to build elevated levels of success for the long term.

Before we dive deeper into how to apply the laws of supply and demand to predict the future of your investment in a business idea, let us unpack the real meaning of some fundamental concepts that the Economics 101 law is built upon.

DEMAND

Formal Definition

"A consumer's desire to purchase a given product or service and their willingness to pay a specific price for that."

Contextual Definition

Demand measures the level of need or want for a particular product or service. It can be measured in terms of how many orders you and your industry have had for your type of offerings in the recent past.

When predicting market timing, we are attempting to forecast demand for your offering in the future by looking at how orders for a product or service in your industry have been trending over time. Then we extrapolate the trendline built on past data to forecast where demand will be at a specified time in the future.

How to Apply

It is very risky for any business to go to market with a new offering without the customer demand for that type of product or service. You would be betting, praying, or hoping that the demand will rise by the time your product is ready to launch.

For all the winning market timing strategies, we would recommend assuming a high demand that remains elevated consistently. Alternatively, another good strategy is based on the demand being established at a relatively low to medium level, but there are strong reasons to believe that it will rapidly increase in the near future.

The only time low or downward trending demand is an acceptable market to enter is when you are creating a small niche lifestyle business because you are a veteran in this sector and are reluctant to learn new skills to venture into a different industry. If you are good at what you do and run a highly efficient operation, you might be able to survive in this market, but do not expect higher levels of success without favorable demand conditions.

The ideal scenario is when demand is much higher than supply/competition, and you possess a competitive advantage in an industry that is difficult to enter.

We highly recommend combining the study of demand trends in your industry with that of external factors, which may induce a change in the customer's level of urgency to purchase your product/ service in the future. Hence, it is very important to ensure that you enter markets where demand grows faster than supply because of an organically strong and sustainable problem urgency.

SUPPLY

Formal Definition

"Make a product or service available to someone or a group of people."

Contextual Definition

The study of supply tells us about the quantity of goods and services available in the market in relation to demand. When predicting market timing, we attempt to forecast the level of competition at a specified time in the future by looking at how the supply has been trending over time. We also determine the extent of the general public's awareness of rising demand and the difficulty of entering a market as another competitor.

How to Apply

As per the laws of economics, when demand is high and sustained, many new suppliers will be entering the market soon to fill the gap. If the knowledge of rising demand is on the front page of a major news channel, then you can safely assume that there is plenty of competition entering the market shortly. The only exception to this rule is evident when the barrier to entering a particular business or industry is very high.

Even if the demand for your type of product or service increases in the market, the requirement for your business's offerings can be impacted by the level of supply or competition in the future.

The ideal market timing to enter would be when the supply of your type of product or service is very low in relation to the demand. In reality, it is very rare, if not impossible, to find opportunities where demand is consistently skyrocketing while the supply remains low.

A bad market timing condition would be when your market is overly crowded and supply is equal to or higher than demand. This is a very competitive scenario that is great for the customer but really bad for businesses, especially for new entrants.

In this type of market, customers know that they have access to a lot of good substitutes. Therefore, they become very price-sensitive and have no incentive to remain loyal to a specific business. Typically, the established large players do well in this condition because they can lower prices through economies of scale and reduce competition via acquisitions or predatory pricing. This is a race to the bottom, and it is best to stay clear of such competitive market timing conditions. Most of the time, markets that are difficult to enter can prove to be highly profitable.

DIFFICULTY OF ENTERING

Formal Definition

"Complexity to overcome obstacles that prevent access to participate in the supply of a product or service in the market."

Contextual Definition

The level of difficulty for new competitors to enter your market and supply similar products or services as you.

How to Apply

Ideally, we want demand to be high, supply to be low, and the difficulty of entering our market to be very high for everyone other than us. In this scenario, we have already overcome the barriers to entry or are highly confident that we have the competitive advantage needed to enter our target market as a supplier effortlessly and swiftly.

It is easy to tell what the supply was in the past or what it is right now. However, predicting supply far out in the future is difficult because other competitors in the making also like to keep their intentions secretive until they are ready to deliver. On the contrary, studying how challenging it is to enter a market is a more objective and data-driven pursuit.

To objectively identify a market that is hard to enter, you must understand the primary factors that strengthen the barriers to entry:

A. Complexity of domain

B. General public awareness is limited—well-kept secret

C. Regulatory requirements

D. Current talent availability is low

E. Limited future talent pool—follow university enrollments in the field

F. Intellectual property—you have a strong and broad patent

G. Well-guarded industry—connection-driven business

H. High cost to start

Once you have a good understanding of these factors, you can follow a step-by-step framework to evaluate how difficult it is to enter your target market.

Step 1: Identify how many of the aforementioned factors apply to the market you want to enter.

Step 2: Score a number between 0 and 10 for each of the factors you have identified. A score of 0 means that the factor doesn't apply at all. On the other hand, a score of 10 implies that the factor is highly applicable to making the market difficult to enter.

Step 3: The higher the cumulative score of the factors influencing the difficulty level, the better it is for you to pursue that market. It works similarly for the number of criteria applicable; more is better. However, it is important to note that this works only if you can acquire a competitive advantage quickly!

The difficulty of entering a market is a good predictor of the future supply/competition in that sector. Entering a market that

is highly challenging to break into is a lucrative proposition if you can develop a competitive advantage in that field.

COMPETITIVE ADVANTAGE

Formal Definition

"A condition or circumstance that puts a person or company in a favorable or superior business position."

Contextual Definition

Competitive advantage refers to the Unique Value Propositions (UVPs) that give you an edge over your competitors in the market when it comes to offering comparable products or services.

How to Apply

Competitive advantage works really well in markets where the existing solutions are stale, and disruption is much needed. Ideally, demand should not be high because if it is so, others will figure out a way to enter that market. When the difficulty of entering is significant, you will have enough runway to make money and grow your competitive advantage through innovation.

Many develop a competitive edge over time by accumulating certain rare skills, experiences, and licenses/certifications in a domain where there aren't many players with similar benefits. Large successful companies invest heavily in R&D and valuable patents to increase their competitive advantage by deterring or completely blocking out future competition! It is important to note that there are too many worthless patents out there, but a well-defined one with broad protection for your innovation can also help you establish a monopoly in the market for a long period.

There are a few cost-effective strategies that anyone can use to build their long-term unique value proposition. Let's take a look at what they entail:

A. You must always prioritize developing expertise over making money. This could be related to a hobby or a side gig in your new target market.

B. It is vital to develop your network and build with the experts in your field. Consider volunteering or interning under a respected leader to gain exposure.

C. You should passively invest in practical R&D for the industry you are targeting. Create valuable intellectual property, and file a patent when you develop innovations worth protecting.

These strategies are best when paired with the following market conditions:

1. Competition is low.

2. Demand is low to medium.

3. You believe this space will be very hot in the next one to three years.

Developing a competitive advantage takes time, and quite often, it does not pay off because either the differential factor isn't significant enough or it's in a market that never gets the expected growth in demand because of low problem urgency.

PROBLEM URGENCY

Formal Definition

"Important matter that requires swift action."

Contextual Definition

The perception your market holds regarding the importance of the problem they are facing and the measure of their impatience to solve it.

How to Apply

The level of urgency your target customers feel for solving a problem they are facing has the tendency to drive up demand in the future.

Predicting future demand based on past trends is a guessing game and hard to do accurately because the trend lines can change at any point in time. However, the demand in the future can be highly impacted by problems that are building up in their level of urgency today.

Fortunately, spotting a problem's urgency for a market is a more data-driven method than forecasting demand and can be repeated consistently by learning the right skills. It can be identified by studying concrete data that is widely available to those who are looking for it. To accurately spot an urgency that has the ability to grow future demand early, we need to understand what causes a problem to become urgent:

A. Mandate-Based Problem Urgency

> A legal, compliance, or security issue that is rapidly growing into a problem and impacts a large enough group that may force the authorities and industry leaders to mandate a set of regulations to address these risks. When a mandate is combined with a set deadline to go into effect, it can surely cause demand to grow in the future as the market becomes aware of this development. A proactive strategy to build demand in your industry is to find such mandates well ahead of their deadline and establish yourself as a leader by making people aware of the upcoming regulatory changes. You can subsequently offer your product or service as a viable solution to their now urgent problem.

B. Pop Culture–Driven Problem Urgency

> Humans are very social, and rapidly growing trends can cause a sense of urgency through peer pressure. Spotting a rising trend early that may become a popular culture in your target industry can give you a head start on finding the growing demand. You must aim to get in early but not too soon. Demand predictions related to this problem urgency work well in markets that are difficult to enter, where the customer base is constantly connected, and peer pressure influence is strong. Some celebrity entrepreneurs like Steve Jobs in the past and Elon Musk in recent times possess the power to create problem urgency because of their influence on pop culture. A smart strategy would be to follow what these celebrity entrepreneurs are doing and try to emulate their move or partner with one of them in your industry.

Strategies for entering a new market based on pop culture–driven problem urgency are only productive in the long term if you can supply a high-quality product with consistency and have the capability to scale rapidly.

C. Survival-Based Problem Urgency

Humans tend to prioritize survival over growth and evolution. When people believe that they have to buy a product or service to survive, they will do whatever it takes to get it. For example, during the recent pandemic, a majority of the population purchased masks and got vaccinated because of the fear of dying, even before the law came into effect. Of course, it took some time and a lot of media attention for the population to become aware of the threat the disease posed. However, once the fear was established, it didn't take much time to create the problem urgency as survival was on the line.

The survival-based problem urgency naturally tops the list of urgencies that can drive up demand. How people reacted when they thought that the world would end just because the Mayan calendar was about to is a prime example of this urgency's dominance.

The Mayans are an ancient civilization from Mexico, and their culture still thrives today in that part of the world. They had invented a pretty impressive calendar system for ancient times, but it did not go beyond 2012. Perhaps for similar reasons that software engineers in the 1900s did not future-proof some of their designs of the most critical computer systems to accommodate for the new millennium— the 2000s. Likewise, it was not a problem for the Mayan calendar founders to solve because 2012 was too far away to be a priority.

Several malicious businesses misused this co-incidental opportunity to propagate their doomsday survival products at a premium to a population segment that was already pessimistic and gullible to believe in their scam. The businesses selling their doomsday kit on this baseless lie might have made a quick profit, but their credibility was totally crushed on January 1, 2013, when the world did not end just because the Mayan calendar ended!

Fear of survival can be a catalyst to create problem urgency, but we must be careful not to misuse this strategy to spike future demand because your credibility will eventually be lost, especially when the problem is not rooted in provable and believable reality. The truth always prevails, and once credibility goes, it is very hard to earn it back.

A better way to build a business without losing credibility is to tap into a market where the demand is growing organically and the competition is very low. This is only possible if you are aware of the different market timing conditions that exist.

The Four Types of Market Timing Conditions

The majority of businesses are surviving instead of thriving because they have yet to learn how to find the right market timing condition. The few who found their way into the zeitgeist before their runway expired have gone on to become household names, such as Google, Facebook, Apple, Microsoft, Amazon, and Tesla.

I have to emphasize that we can only talk in terms of probabilities when it comes to market timing because there are no guarantees when predicting the future. All predictions come with their expiration dates. Even the best predictions are only valid in the time frame for which they were made. Therefore, it is very important to focus on the "timing" part because market conditions can change over time without explicit notice.

For example, thirty years ago, investing in the electric vehicle industry would have been a losing proposition. However, in the past ten years, the electric car segment has become a good investment opportunity because the market conditions have evolved.

Tesla took advantage of this major shift in market conditions early on. It wasn't an easy journey, but today they are by far the most valuable car company in the world and one of the largest enterprises out there by market cap value. What is a bad industry to invest in at a given time frame can become a favorable investment in another period and vice versa.

In this chapter, we will only dive deeper into the two winning market timing strategies. I refer to them as the winning ones because, among the four market timing conditions, only two offer a high-enough success probability to justify the inherent risk of innovating a new product or service. The other two strategies carry a much higher risk of failure. However, it is equally important to learn about the wrong strategies so that you can tell the good from the bad early and fast.

Let's revisit the four different market timing strategies (introduced in chapter 3) visually before we take a deep dive into each of these.

Market Timing Strategy #1: Greenfield Market—"The Zeitgeist"

When your dream aligns perfectly with the spirit and mood of the era, your odds of winning are significantly higher before you even get started. If your idea is executed and brought to life at a time when the mood is in transition, and the market is just getting ready to accept what you have to offer, then we call that perfect timing.

Tapping into "the Zeitgeist" is a winning market timing strategy that holds the highest probability of success that can only exist in a Greenfield state.

A **Greenfield market** condition is when demand for your type of product or service ranges from high to very high and the supply/competition is low. This "golden gap" circumstance does not often occur in today's overly populated, highly educated, and hyper-connected world. The zeitgeist is always hiding in plain sight, like a needle in a haystack, along with all the fads of its time.

Here's a graphical representation of what a Greenfield market looks like:

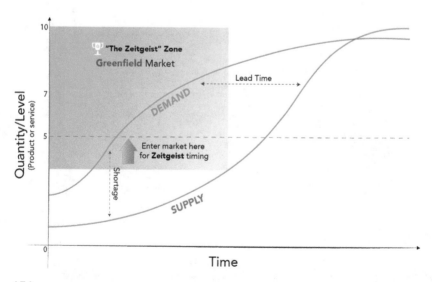

In a Greenfield market:

A. Demand is medium and rising rapidly or

B. Demand is already high and expected to grow continuously in the near future; and

C. Supply remains low, and the big potential competitors aren't paying attention yet.

Greenfield markets should not necessarily be difficult to enter because when the tide is rising, all boats can rise as long as there aren't too many near one another, which can lead to a crash. For the same reason, it is not as important to possess a major competitive advantage in this market condition as it would be in others.

You just have to offer a decent product or service that will bring value to your customers as quickly as possible. However, in the long term, it is highly lucrative to establish yourself with a major competitive advantage in markets that are difficult to enter. Doing so significantly increases the longevity of the Greenfield market.

TAPPING INTO THE ZEITGEIST— WINNING STRATEGY

You must accept the hard truth that all Greenfield markets will eventually turn into Redfield. However, you can certainly make the most of this condition if you have the right plan in place. Here's how you can tap into the zeitgeist with this winning market timing strategy:

1. Confirm that your idea is in a Greenfield market condition.

2. Demand should be medium and not too high but growing fast when you enter. (Refer to the "Zeitgeist Zone" arrow in the Greenfield market graph.)

3. The market that you are targeting is still a niche, and the masses are not paying attention to it.

4. Ensure that the major technical breakthroughs needed to develop your idea have been achieved and that you have access to develop on top of those advancements.

5. Make sure that you have the competitive advantage needed to execute your idea because markets don't remain Greenfield for a long time.

6. The supplier and distributor ecosystem that you will need to successfully venture into your market should be mature enough and ready to support your success when you plan to scale the business.

It is important to get the timing right if you want a good shot at tapping into the zeitgeist within its window of opportunity because the Greenfield market can become crowded with competition and turn into a Redfield state.

Market Timing Strategy #2: Redfield Market—"The Disruptor"

The majority of players like to play it safe because of the fear of failing, and they end up waiting too long to execute their grand idea. Unfortunately, they don't get to enjoy extraordinary returns because the market changes into a Redfield state by the time they execute on their vision. This happens more often than not because it is nearly impossible to know whether you have tapped into the zeitgeist unless you have the right tools.

In a *Redfield market*, both demand and supply for a product or service are red hot. However, the demand still maintains a lead, and there is some room for new players to grow. This market can appeal to many despite the risk of intense competition because you can build a successful business faster and more efficiently by learning from the mistakes of competitors who paved the way before you.

Another important advantage of doing business in the Redfield state is market awareness. Educating the target customers about your product or service is a very expensive process, which has already been done by the pioneers of the industry. However, because of the intense level of competition, you need to have a very good wow factor and amazing execution ability to even stand a chance of winning in this condition.

Here's a graphical representation of what a Redfield market looks like:

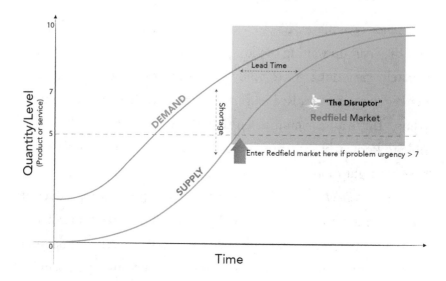

In a Redfield market:

A. Demand ranges from high to very high and is expected to grow further

B. Supply is high, and the space is quite competitive

C. Supply is relatively lower than demand

Most Redfields eventually evolve into Deadfield markets when the demand saturates with an overcrowded pool of competitors. Occasionally, a major disruptor enters and clears the field by putting all the competition out of business through an unmatchable wow factor that evolves the market. Such events are pretty rare because it is very difficult to turn around an industry, but when they happen, a Redfield is recycled into a Greenfield state.

Redfield markets, where the demand boom is relatively young and customer satisfaction is low, can be an excellent opportunity for cost-effective disruption despite having too many established players.

THE DISRUPTOR—WINNING STRATEGY

Established red-hot markets with high customer dissatisfaction and low customer loyalty are great opportunities for a disruptor with a significant competitive advantage to enter and solve these challenges. In this scenario, the established competition is busy focusing on revenue and profits, while the disruptor ventures in without the trials and tribulations of the early movers. They can solely focus on offering a delightful and unparalleled customer experience that people would really appreciate.

In addition to the Redfield conditions, the disruptor market has the following characteristics:

1. Customer satisfaction is low, and the problem urgency of the market is high (greater than 7 out of 10).

2. Customer loyalty toward the existing established players is low.

3. No individual competitor owns at least 40 percent of the market share, with high customer satisfaction and rapid growth in capturing new demand.

4. Nobody else has a patent or intellectual property advantage that would block new entrants.

5. The level of "difficulty to enter" for new players is relatively high.

6. The cost to enter the market is not exorbitantly high for you.

As a rule of thumb, you should always be very reluctant to invest in a Redfield market idea even if you strongly feel that you can be "the Disruptor."

There are always exceptions to every rule. Not all Redfield markets are bad. Sometimes it may be so crowded that everyone is busy competing for revenue and other short-term goals to the extent that they miss the bigger underlying problems that cause major market inefficiencies.

Google is a great example of a disruptive startup that entered a Redfield market and eventually put all the established players out of business. They entered the search engine space toward the end of the dot-com boom (the late 1990s), competing with well-established giants such as Yahoo, Altavista, AOL, and a dozen other search engine platforms. You might remember this if you were old enough to be on the Internet back then.

Back in the 1990s, search engine users were very dissatisfied. Google's competitors at the time emulated the TV model, where they approached the market as if the advertisers paying them money were the real customers instead of the actual search engine users they served. So there was no customer loyalty because of how poorly the products on the market addressed the user's critical pain points. Hence, it was a market screaming for a product that could deliver a superior customer experience.

Google addressed these problems and became a disruptor in the search engine industry. They came in with a unique approach to address what the search users wanted and captured the market so well that they are now essentially a monopoly two decades later.

Timing disruptive opportunities in a Redfield market is very difficult if you are an outsider, but it is probably even harder as an insider. It can be challenging to think outside the box if you are

biased and limited in vision by the surroundings you have been in for a long time.

Tesla is another good example of a major disruptor in the Redfield market. The car industry was already well established when Tesla decided to enter the market with an all-electric smart car option. All the major established car manufacturers had an electric car offering, but it was niche and not very functional. Tesla's founders (not Elon Musk) envisioned a world where vehicles were not just modern looking and equipped with smart features but also fully electric. However, they went on a very technically challenging journey. The supply chain and distribution hurdles were so enormous that Tesla's founders ran out of funds. This forced them to hand over the company's control to a visionary like Elon Musk, who was an early investor in the business.

Elon Musk saw a rapidly changing customer need for cars in the new millennium. People had rising concerns about the impact of carbon emissions on the environment and a heightened awareness of the effects of climate change on our future. The public was also growing an appetite for smarter cars with advanced technology that would make driving easier than ever. The Tesla team eventually delivered a highly disruptive product that led them to become the industry leader in the electric car market and also the most valuable car company on the planet.

As a result of Elon Musk's breakthrough in delivering a viable product and his efforts as a celebrity entrepreneur to patiently build market demand, the electric automobile industry is now in a Greenfield state. The demand for electric cars is high and growing, with many new players entering the market relatively easily and successfully. The market is in a state where all boats can rise!

Not all startups entering a Redfield market are going to be "The Disruptor."

The following are some common signs to evaluate your odds of disrupting a Redfield market:

A. Your approach happens to be very innovative and much better than the competition.

B. Your ability to execute in this market is impeccable.

C. The level of difficulty to enter for new players is relatively high

D. You have a significant competitive advantage as a disruptor that will be hard for the established players to copy.

E. You have a cost-effective and highly scalable market expansion strategy.

F. You have managed to keep your unique approach to the market secretive, and there aren't any competitors launching a similar offering in the same time frame.

Entrepreneurs tend to be very passionate, and they get emotionally attached to their ideas. Therefore, it is very important to objectively assess your chances of being the disrupter to viably enter a Redfield market.

Market Timing #3: Brownfield Market—"Eventual Potential"

Being early with your market timing in an area where demand is growing is good. However, entering too early could also mean that the market may not be ready to adopt your idea at a scale to turn it into a viable business anytime soon. You may need to be extremely patient, execute well, and have sufficient funds to wait for the market and partner ecosystem to embrace your idea. This is what we call a **Brownfield market**—"Eventual Potential."

This is a special market timing category, with many companies whose names you may not have heard before. However, they are noteworthy because they have silently left a mark on the world with their significant innovative contributions despite experiencing massive commercial failure. These types of companies mostly fail to succeed because they enter eventual potential markets way too early, but they set the stage for future super-successful businesses.

Here's a graphical representation of what a Brownfield market looks like:

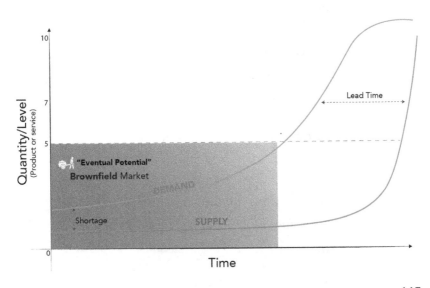

Sometimes, Brownfield markets can also look like this:

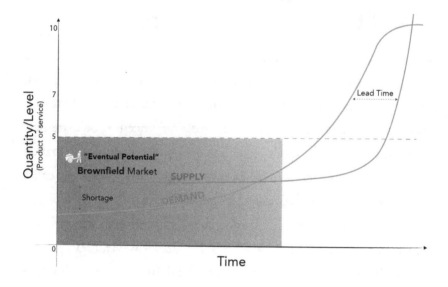

In a Brownfield market:

1. Demand is low

2. Supply is low

3. Demand can be higher than supply or vice versa

4. It's highly speculative

There is no established demand-supply trend in this market condition, making it impossible to predict whether there will be a boom or not. Markets typically remain in the Brownfield state because

    a. The demand isn't ready for this solution yet.

or

    b. No viable solutions are available at the time to serve the demand because of extreme technical difficulties. This also keeps the demand low.

or

c. The supply chain and distribution ecosystem needed for your success is not mature enough or unwilling to support your go-to market plan.

Very few celebrity entrepreneurs have the ability to build demand after entering a Brownfield market. Even the publicity stunt–generated demand isn't sustainable if the organic need from customers is almost negligible, and the ecosystem needed to distribute your product is unavailable to provide the support necessary to uphold the momentum.

As seen in the case study from chapter 2, General Magic is a good example of a failed Brownfield market player. The 100 percent renewable energy solution for homes is another good example of this category that has yet to evolve into a Greenfield state. Solar technology has been around for years, but it is quite expensive and not that effective practically for a wide range of applications. It is only commercially viable because of government incentives to promote renewable energy. Even Tesla's effort in this space with the solar city and roof material has experienced massive technological obstacles in bringing a viable product to the market.

I strongly recommend NOT to enter Brownfield markets as it is not a winning strategy. Entering in this market condition is a gamble because you may succeed eventually if you have a solid breakthrough, but most likely, you will die trying.

Only enter a Brownfield market if:

A. You have a deep passion for solving the problem that the market is struggling with.

B. You have a competitive advantage and the right technical resources to stand a chance at a breakthrough.

C. You have an influence on the market, or you partnered with someone who can create market demand by the time your product launches.

D. You have impeccable execution capability.

E. You are very well-funded and have the patience and focus to play the long game.

F. You can stick by a deadline to achieve the breakthroughs necessary to continue.

G. You can afford to lose everything you have invested.

People often venture into a Brownfield market thinking they are early movers in a Greenfield condition. In most cases, they are forced to give up on their dreams because of the massive failures they encounter early on in this journey. Therefore, spotting the difference between these two market timing strategies is paramount.

BROWNFIELD VERSUS GREENFIELD

Brownfield markets often disguise themselves as Greenfields. In your excitement and passion for the business idea, it is very easy to miss all the signs that would have helped you detect a Brownfield, giving you the illusion of being the next zeitgeist.

It can be very easy to misread these two market timing conditions because they can look very similar. What clearly differentiates them is knowing (1) how established is the true demand and (2) the strength of the actual demand trend. In a Greenfield market, you are moving in early but not too soon. On the other hand, in a Brownfield condition, you may be moving well ahead of time. To be clear, I do not recommend being a very early mover. Usually, venturing into a market very early comes with high levels of risks. These risk-takers are what we call "the Pioneers."

Pioneers take on the great burden of market discovery by solving the hard customer awareness and technology problems. In the end, they often run out of their runway before they are able to launch a viable consumer-grade product/service whose demand really picks up. They also pave the way for the second or third mover with strong execution discipline to come in and tap into the zeitgeist.

Apple's iPhone under Steve Jobs is a good example of this. General Magic did all the impossible R&D as the first mover before they ran out of funds and eventually went bankrupt. Steve Jobs then built on the momentum established by General Magic and launched a phenomenal product with unmatched execution discipline, and it simply tapped into the zeitgeist like very few innovations have done in the past.

The same can be said about Myspace and Facebook. In this case, Myspace was the first mover, and Facebook simply had great timing as a second-mover, but they were still early enough to hit a home run. Myspace became distracted after its acquisition, and Facebook benefited immensely from this opportunity.

The following are the most common warning signs that will help you in differentiating a Brownfield from a Greenfield market:

1. The demand for your solution is all hype and no reality. The best sign of this is when you pitch your hypothetical offering to the target day 1 customers, and they show no interest in talking to you or buying what you have to offer. This is why market testing during the early ideation phase is extremely critical to avoid misreading your market timing condition. Refer to chapter 10 on how to test whether there is genuine demand for your offering with your target market.

2. You are unable to find any significant competitors offering or building something similar to your business idea. This is a sign that there may be no demand for your type of solution, or the problem is way too hard to solve, so nobody wants to enter the market at this stage. It's too early.

3. You face grave technical difficulties in finding component suppliers or open-source libraries. As a result, you have to create basic building blocks for your product from scratch, which can take a very long time.

4. The underlying ecosystem that you need to distribute your product is nonexistent, and the partners you rely on for your go-to market are not interested in building their capabilities to support your success.

BROWNFIELD TO GREENFIELD

Most companies in the Brownfield market fail to achieve their vision but pave the way for others to succeed. However, there are some who don't take no for an answer and do see the light at the end of the tunnel. Tesla, in the electric vehicle industry, is a great example of a player who turned a Brownfield market into a Greenfield state.

While the car market has been Redfield or highly competitive for decades now, if we look at a sub-segment of this industry, the electric vehicle market, we can say it was in a Brownfield state until 2017. With the launch of the Tesla Model 3, the electric car segment evolved to a level where their products became accessible and affordable to the mainstream population.

Prior to Tesla's breakthrough in this industry, many established car manufacturers, such as Toyota and GM, had been trying to launch a viable product since the early 2000s. There were two major engineering challenges faced by all the players. First, the range for the existing electric car was not long enough for it to be a viable product. Second, making fast charging accessible to car owners needed a lot of investment in developing the right infrastructure.

Tesla was founded in 2003, but it did not launch its first car, the Roadster, until 2008. It took them a change in ownership and major investments to build a good product at a price point affordable enough to go Greenfield fourteen years after their inception. Interestingly, Tesla didn't turn profitable until 2020. However, after surpassing the breakeven point, they went on a journey of exponential growth. This winning spree led them to become the most valuable car company on the planet by market value, eventually earning the title of "the richest person on the planet" for its visionary and resilient CEO.

The company's trials and tribulations were funded for seventeen years by its famous CEO and other investors. Their resilience and commitment helped them turn a Brownfield market into a Greenfield one, which is a very rare occurrence. This is how Tesla tapped into the "Golden Gap" opportunity in the electric vehicle industry early on and was able to succeed faster.

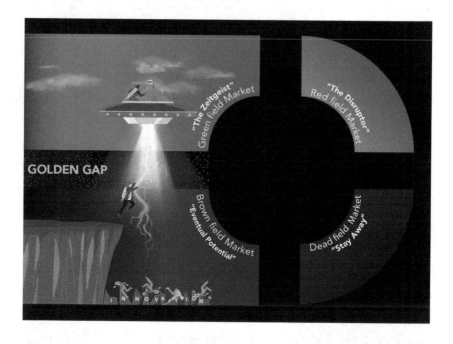

Golden Gap Concept

Market Timing #4: Deadfield Market—"Stay Away"

In a **Deadfield market**, the demand for a given product or service is either saturated or dying, and the supply is high with many established competitors already in the field. This is a very risky market condition, and I would advise you to **stay away** from investing in such business ideas.

Once you know that your business idea involves a higher risk, you can either "stay away" from this opportunity or move forward knowing what's at stake for a very good personal reason. Maybe your business is the only profession that you know, and you are not willing to start all over to discover a new market. Perhaps you have a deep passion for your industry or a strong personal desire that compels you to venture in such high-risk markets.

If you decide to pursue one of the two high-risk market timing strategies, consider it a gamble, and only put in the time and effort that you are prepared to lose.

Here's a graphical representation of what a Deadfield market always looks like:

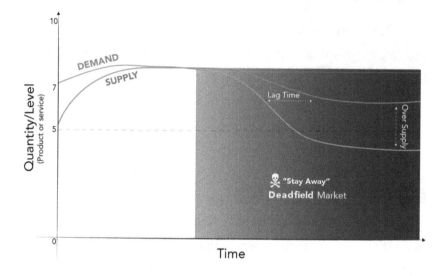

In a Deadfield market:

A. Demand is saturated/flat lined or falling

B. Supply is higher than or equal to demand

C. Mostly, there is an oversupply of products or services

D. Product offerings are mature, and customers are satisfied with the solutions

A good example of the Deadfield market timing is the video cassette and DVD rental market in the 2000s. During this period, the explosion of online video streaming services like YouTube and Netflix caused the video DVD and cassette rental industry to quickly turn a Redfield market into a Deadfield one. This led to the rapid demise of major players in the industry, including Blockbuster and Hollywood Video.

However, Netflix managed to tap into the zeitgeist by introducing an amazing online video streaming service in 2007. They pivoted out of this dying industry and entered into a Greenfield state. At this time, the market was looking for more on-demand and highly convenient digital video-based content. Why now? Because there were major underlying ecosystem changes happening in the mid-2000s that helped digital content service providers to flourish. The widespread availability of Internet-based TVs, smartphones with high-quality displays, and high-speed wireless Internet at home were some of the most significant changes that happened during this period.

Powerful new entrants, such as Redbox, emerged around the same time as Netflix but failed to succeed despite their innovative approach. They even employed self-service kiosk technologies to rent video DVDs and CDs at many high-traffic stores, but it was not that successful. They were not able to succeed despite being founded and fully backed by the fast-food giant McDonald's. In August 2022, the Redbox business was acquired by a company named Chicken Soup for the Soul Entertainment.

You should only enter or stay in the Deadfield market if you are an established player focusing on building innovative products to gain a competitive advantage. Also, you must make your operation extremely efficient and consolidate it by acquiring competitors who are capturing new market share.

MARKET TIMING LIFE CYCLE

Market timing conditions do not stay constant for a long period. Like everything else in this world, these conditions evolve, transform, and sometimes even reset. It is important to note that all market timing assessments are only valid within the time frame for which the prediction was made. Markets go through different phases, and in the long term, they tend to follow a life cycle pattern. They can transform from Brownfield to Greenfield and eventually mature into a Redfield to finally end in a Deadfield state.

Here is a graphical representation of how market timing conditions evolve:

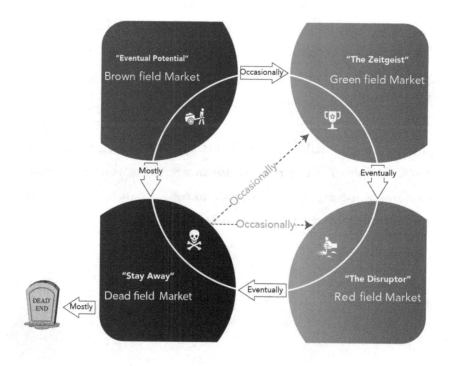

The progression of a typical market timing life cycle is as follows:

1. It starts at Brownfield for a new market offering.

2. The Brownfield mostly turns into a Deadfield market.

3. Occasionally, Brownfield markets get transformed into Greenfields by disruptors. For example, the electric vehicle industry in 2015.

4. Greenfield markets eventually evolve into Redfield ones when competition increases.

5. Most Redfields eventually saturate into Deadfield markets. For example, Blockbuster.

   Video cassette and DVD rentals turned Deadfield after 2007 as some market players, such as Netflix, evolved into a Greenfield state with digital video streaming services. Today, the video streaming market has become Redfield again with a high level of competition growing along with rising demand.

6. The Deadfield markets can occasionally transform when there is a mandate or survival-based problem urgency. For example, the facial mask market in the United States was pretty dead prior to the COVID-19 pandemic. The supply was very established and mature, but sales were saturated before the pandemic. Due to the rapid spread of the virus in 2020, the demand for masks rose astronomically and turned this market into a Greenfield state.

Studying the market timing life cycle provides us deeper insights into the importance of timing for the success of any business idea. What is trending today might become obsolete in the next few months and vice versa. Therefore, it is essential to validate the alignment of your idea with the zeitgeist of your era. As promised in the beginning of this chapter, we will now introduce you to the most awaited and invaluable tools to tap into the zeitgeist: the Zeitgeist Prediction Worksheet and the Zeitgeist Predictive Model!

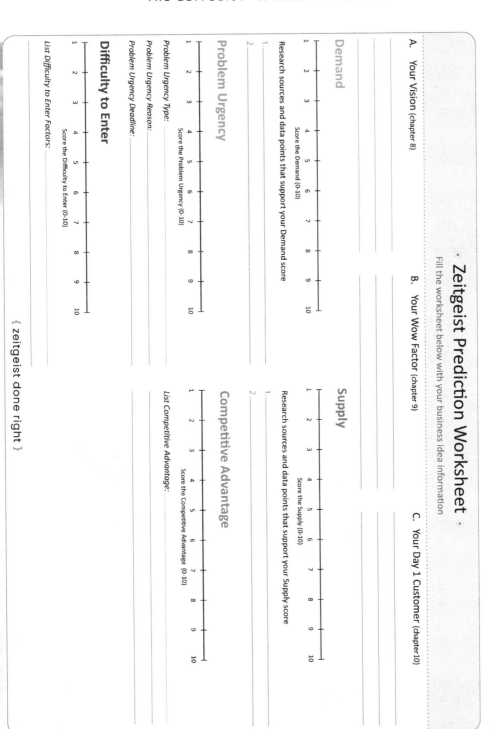

Zeitgeist Prediction Worksheet

Fill the worksheet below with your business idea information

A. Your Vision (chapter 8)

B. Your Wow Factor (chapter 9)

C. Your Day 1 Customer (chapter10)

Demand

1 2 3 4 5 6 7 8 9 10

Score the Demand (0-10)

Research sources and data points that support your Demand score

1.

2.

Problem Urgency

1 2 3 4 5 6 7 8 9 10

Score the Problem Urgency (0-10)

Problem Urgency Type:

Problem Urgency Reason:

Problem Urgency Deadline:

Difficulty to Enter

1 2 3 4 5 6 7 8 9 10

Score the Difficulty to Enter (0-10)

List Difficulty to Enter Factors:

Supply

1 2 3 4 5 6 7 8 9 10

Score the Supply (0-10)

Research sources and data points that support your Supply score

1.

2.

Competitive Advantage

1 2 3 4 5 6 7 8 9 10

Score the Competitive Advantage (0-10)

List Competitive Advantage:

{ zeitgeist done right }

179

Zeitgeist Predictive Model

Get your Market Timing right!

HOW TO USE

Step 1: Plot Your Scores

Plot the demand and supply scores from the detachable Zeitgeist Predictive Worksheet (previous page) on the Zeitgeist Predictive Matrix (next page).

Step 2: Interpret the Zeitgeist Model

A. If your idea fits in the Greenfield box, it suggests that your market timing is right and you should proceed to step 3. The further to the top left you fit on the matrix, the higher the probability that you have tapped into a zeitgeist.

B. If you fit in the Redfield—Disrupt the Status Quo box in the top right quadrant, then you should consider the market timing to be aligned only if the problem urgency score is 7 or greater. For this category, your probability of success as a disrupter is higher because the problem urgency gets closer to 10. This indicates that, while your customers have a lot of choices, their pain point is so high that they would be easily willing to get onboard if you address their urgent problem correctly.

Step 3: Proceed to the next level of research and idea testing
The Wow Factor and Day-1 Customer Discovery (Next 3 chapters).

Zeitgeist Predictive Matrix for Plotting

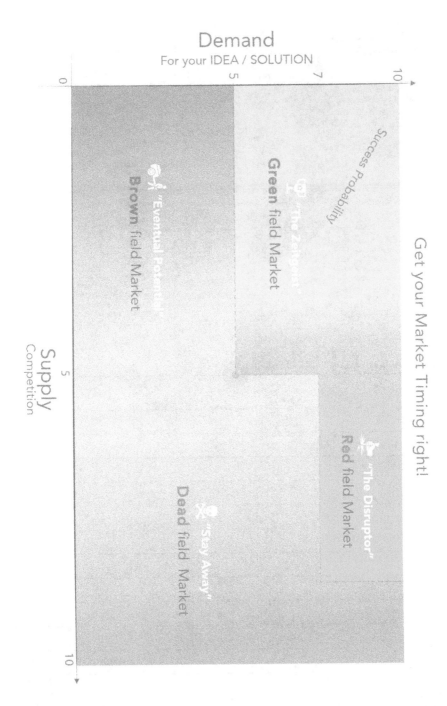

CHAPTER 7 – KEY TAKEAWAYS

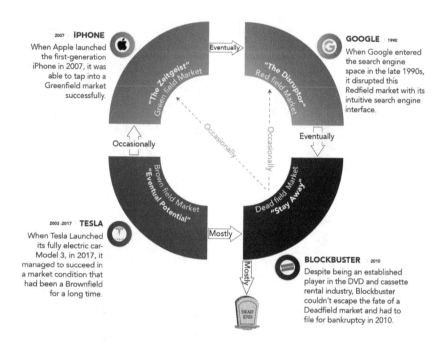

2007 iPHONE
When Apple launched the first-generation iPhone in 2007, it was able to tap into a Greenfield market successfully.

GOOGLE 1990
When Google entered the search engine space in the late 1990s, it disrupted this Redfield market with its intuitive search engine interface.

2003 -2017 TESLA
When Tesla Launched its fully electric car-Model 3, in 2017, it managed to succeed in a market condition that had been a Brownfield for a long time.

BLOCKBUSTER 2010
Despite being an established player in the DVD and cassette rental industry, Blockbuster couldn't escape the fate of a Deadfield market and had to file for bankruptcy in 2010.

YOUR NOTES

PART II

THE SUCCEED-FASTER METHOD

*Learn the **methods** required to help you plan how to succeed faster and win consistently before investing in building your idea.*

What Is Your Wow Factor?

Do not waste money building anything until you can clearly articulate your most valuable feature that wows your day 1 customers!

CHAPTER 8

THE "WOW" FACTOR

There is a billion-dollar question that has been on my mind for the past seven years. How can we build great things that we dream of without having to fail repeatedly before maybe one day we pivot our way to success after spending years, decades, or even a lifetime? The answer to this billion-dollar question is hidden inside what I call the "wow factor."

When the day 1 customers and the wow factors are identified up front correctly, great things happen faster and cheaper, with minimal pivots and painful failures along the way.

In chapter 3, we explored the importance of tapping into the zeitgeist when ideating a product or service before taking them to market. As amazing as the zeitgeist is, it alone cannot give you an ultra-close-up view of what problem to solve for your market. It lacks the specific understanding of your unique value proposition that will wow your day 1 target audience.

The zeitgeist is a high-level map that guides you broadly in a direction that will help you get the success that you desire. It is like looking at a world map and focusing on the continent and the country where you want to go. That is a good start, but you cannot embark on such a journey without knowing exactly which city and airport in that country you want to fly to.

Likewise, when ideating your product or service, you must ensure that you are in the right industry, with perfect market alignment in terms of timing to maximize your odds of winning. However, such a high-level plan is not specific and practical enough for you to start executing to achieve something meaningful. So, do not waste your time and money executing your idea until your day 1 customers are truly inspired when you clearly articulate your wow factor to them! Very few get lucky and win, but everybody else ends up losing in the absence of a clearly defined wow factor!

If the zeitgeist is like a compass telling you whether you are going in the right high-level direction, then the Wow Factor is the zoomed-in view of the map with the exact coordinates of where and how your product/service should land in the market you have chosen.

In this chapter and the next, you will learn exactly what a wow factor is and the process of finding it in a data-driven manner so that you can maximize your probability of success even before starting the journey toward your destination. Before we dive into the intricacies of the wow factor, let's look at an interesting case study on what happens when you don't have one.

No Wow Factor, No Success: A Case Study

Wow factors are critical for the success of your business, and this case study is a strong testament to the fact that not having or identifying the wow factor can lead to abysmal failures.

Yahoo's wild market performance in the past three decades is a great case study taught in MBA programs across business schools globally for what not to do after your company becomes an overnight success story.

The story of Yahoo is quite fascinating because they accidentally stumbled across the zeitgeist of their era during the early days of the Internet boom. The founders of Yahoo, Jerry Yang and David Filo, were college buddies who kept a list of websites by category for their personal use before Internet browsers and search engines were a thing. Even though the founders had no intentions of making this hobby a business, their list went viral across the Internet so quickly that they could not maintain the cost of keeping it up without commercializing. While completely unintentional, the timing was absolutely perfect!

Yahoo was founded as an Internet startup in 1994, right at the dawn of the Internet boom, a time when the technology industry was bursting with possibilities and boundless potential. It was an era characterized by rapid advancements and a sense of uncharted territory as the Internet began to shape the world in ways previously unimaginable. During this period, the Internet was still in its infancy, and the concept of online search and information retrieval was just starting to take shape. The digital landscape was fragmented, with numerous websites emerging and evolving at a remarkable pace. The Internet was primarily used by tech-savvy individuals, and the vast majority of the population had yet to fully grasp its transformative power.

Amid this backdrop of possibility, Yahoo emerged as one of the early pioneers and darlings of the Internet industry. Its ascent mirrored the wild growth of the technology sector, captivating people with its user-friendly interface, comprehensive directory, and the promise of a new era of information accessibility.

By 1999, Yahoo had grown exponentially in all kinds of directions in a span of just four years. From web search engines like Net Controls to web hosting service providers like GeoCities, Yahoo acquired numerous startups in its prime. It paid a whopping $3.5 billion to purchase GeoCities in May 1999. At this point, Yahoo was an Internet giant and an industry leader with a peak market valuation of $125 billion. They were one of the first unicorns (startups worth over a billion dollars) from the Internet bubble era and among the top fifty most valuable companies in the world. The quick and monumental success achieved by Yahoo allowed them to reinvest their capital and grow a vast array of new products. This rapid multifaceted growth made it hard for the Yahoo team to articulate their unique value proposition.

Internal surveys were starting to show signs that Yahoo was losing focus. Their own employees could not agree on one unanimous wow factor that the brand Yahoo stood for. Some thought it was an Internet listing company; others said it was an Internet search engine, an email business, a digital news platform, and a stock reasearch website. They clearly lost their wow factor as the employees could not agree on what the company was really good at!

When a business loses its wow factor, it is the beginning of the end, regardless of its size!

Undoubtedly, the year 1999 was the beginning of the end for Yahoo because they had no wow factor. Yahoo gradually descended from the top into a slow death spiral, ultimately losing 95 percent of its market value by 2014 before it was desperately sold to the telco giant Verizon for $4.8 billion in 2017. The quest to launch a wide range of new products turned out to be a fateful one for Yahoo because they failed to hone and market their wow factor.

Only Hindsight Can Be Twenty-Twenty with Wow Factors

When Yahoo was among the top fifty most valuable companies globally during its prime, it became a magnet for tech startups looking for capital. In this period, Yahoo executives were busy acquiring dozens of new tech businesses to increase their product offerings. One such startup that pitched to Yahoo was a little company called Google, founded by two Stanford University students, Sergey Brin and Larry Page. The executives who had the responsibility and authority to invest in startups did not consider Google as a potential investment option, even though the asking price was only $1 million. The leaders at Yahoo felt that the name Google was very weird. In addition, they did not like the fact that it was too simplistic, with only one feature on their website or rather a blank web page: a search box. That was it, and it remains that way even after twenty-five years!

Back in the 1990s, more was considered better. It was trendy for successful Internet platforms like Yahoo to be crowded with a lot of information, links, and other elements. During that period, websites were more like the digital version of Yellow Pages. Google's wow factor was that they made Internet search fast and easy for users by instantly showing them specific website results that contained highly relevant information to the keywords entered in the search box. The simplicity of Google's website and the singular focus was their genius wow factor.

In the next three years, Google grew exponentially despite a major downturn in the Internet industry. In 2002, Yahoo had the opportunity to buy Google again, but this time, the asking price was 1,000 times higher than the initial one, at $1 billion. They were reluctantly considering the deal. In the next few months, when Jerry Yang, Yahoo's co-founder and CEO, made an offer, Google had already upped their price to $3 billion. They could not afford this price tag as Yahoo was worth only $10 billion by 2002.

The Internet giant Yahoo had lost most of its value fifteen years after its peak. On the other hand, the $1 million startup named Google became a monopoly in the Internet space and now has a market cap of over $1.5 trillion (2023). In hindsight, it is very easy to see why Yahoo should have bought Google for a nominal $1 million when it had an opportunity to do so because Google had a very focused and crystal-clear wow factor that aligned with the evolving zeitgeist. However, it wasn't that obvious back in Yahoo's heyday when it was considering hundreds of other new companies. With all the noise of other exciting and shiny Silicon Valley startups, I am not sure if it would have been that easy to differentiate between the winning and the losing wow factors. Only with luck or a predictive system like the one we will introduce in this chapter is it possible to pick the winning wow feature while looking forward to the future.

The Four Levels of Ideation

It is true that only hindsight can be twenty-twenty with the wow factors. However, you can definitely get close to finding your wow element by ideating through different levels until you come across the feature that would be the most valuable one to take to your market. Ideation is the process of coming up with new ideas or concepts, and while doing so, you can come up with ideas at different levels of detail. Some of them might be very broad to quickly execute, whereas others can be highly specific, allowing you to tap into the opportunities easily, like the product's features.

A feature is a form of an idea communicated at a level of detail that allows the experts to start developing something concrete. At the same time, the idea must be communicated in a form that is easy to comprehend so that anybody reading it can understand exactly what problem it is solving, regardless of their level of expertise in the field. Likewise, a wow factor is very similar to a feature because it's also usually defined at the same level and communicates to both the general public and the experts simultaneously. The wow factor can also be called the most valuable feature (MVF). Remember this term because it will be used interchangeably for "wow factor" throughout this book.

While the wow factor is the most important form of any idea that will allow you to build your business, you must NOT start with the sole purpose of finding it in the first place. That is because there are two higher levels of ideas that exist above the MVF. You need to ensure that the chosen wow factor is well aligned with the higher-level ideas that it stems from. Theoretically, you could come up with an MVF to build your business on, even in a vacuum, where it does not align with the higher-level ideas such as the zeitgeist. However, that is a spray-and-pray strategy that you only follow if you are a very lucky person or don't have the knowledge on how to go about building a business methodically.

I may not be able to help you address the luck part, but let's fix the knowledge gap so that you do not have to rely on luck anymore. In the next chapter, we will learn how to choose a wow factor to build your business. As a prerequisite, we need to first understand the four different levels of ideas that exist.

The Four Levels of Ideation

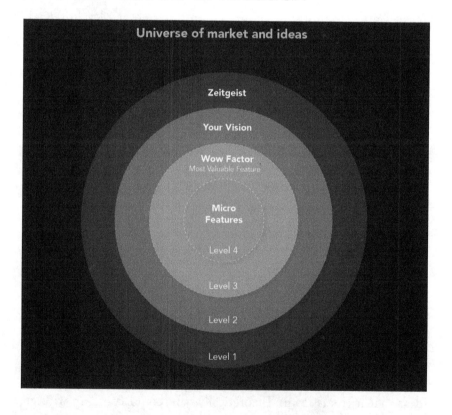

LEVEL 1—ZEITGEIST

The universe of all markets, industries, and ideas out there is very vast, big enough for the entire humanity and more to prosper. However, if you attempt to ideate at this level, it is easy to get lost and confused because of its diversity and limitless possibilities. Therefore, we must aim to start with the next level of ideation that is represented by the zeitgeist, a megatrend in a specific field or market that you can do business in.

It is the first meaningful level where you can ideate. This stage of ideation will help you discover a viable path to success for achieving your business aspirations. At any given time, several zeitgeists could co-exist across different domains and regions in the world. You must be ultra-focused in a specific field to achieve anything meaningful in life. It should be to the extent where you become an expert at minimum or the very best on the upside in a field of your choice.

The zeitgeist happens to be an industry where there is tremendous growth in customer demand but not enough experts who can supply what the market wants. Therefore, if you have to pick a field to focus on, it's best to pick one that is well aligned with the spirit and mood of the era so that you can leverage the tailwind of the entire market. Regardless of whether the field you picked is aligned with the zeitgeist or not, you still have to focus intensively and put in the effort to build your expertise in delivering a viable solution for your chosen market. As long as you are willing to do that, the powerful market forces will help maximize your chances of success.

Let's look at some examples of the zeitgeist:

1. The Internet boom in the 1990s

2. Digitization of commerce with e-commerce in the 2000s

3. Work and social life goes digital on mobile—in the 2010s

4. On-demand streaming of video content in the 2010s

5. Sustainable energy: shift to electric vehicles in the 2020s

6. AI on Cloud and Robotics to fill the labor gap and declining birth rate in the 2020s

The life span of a zeitgeist can be anywhere from seven to twenty years.

That is generally how long a megatrend can last with a sustained demand explosion without competition crowding in. Depending on the difficulty of entering into a field, you can enjoy market tailwinds for a good decade if you tap into a megatrend early enough.

While it is a must to figure out your zeitgeist, you should not start building your business right after picking one because it is an idea that exists in a very broad form. It is practically impossible for a person or a business to know exactly what to build at this stage. At this level, you have only defined what market trend and field you want to play in. It is way too broad of an idea for a meaningful execution. So, you need to go to the next level to get one step closer to defining precisely what you need to build to achieve your goals.

LEVEL 2—YOUR VISION

Your vision is a crystal-clear definition of your business goal at the end point when you reach the destination of your dreams. A strong vision that stems from the zeitgeist that you selected for your business will help you stay focused amid all the noise and distractions that will come your way on the nonlinear, long, and hard road to success. In other words, your vision has to significantly contribute to your chosen field and be highly correlated to the mission of the zeitgeist. In practice, you can pick a vision that is not highly correlated and doesn't make significant valuable contributions to your field. However, that will not help you align your plan to succeed faster and win often.

Vision is the second level of ideation that will lead you one step closer to your destination after you have selected your zeitgeist. It is a powerful compass that points you in the right direction and keeps you focused on where you want to go. A strong vision is ambitious but achievable, specific, long-term, and aligned with the spirit and mood of the era. However, as good as your vision may be, it is still not at a level of sufficient detail to jump into the execution phase. Nonetheless, you should NEVER begin the journey of building a business without a strong vision in place if you want to achieve your goals in the least amount of time possible.

The typical life span of a vision is between one and five years.

Generally, an ambitious-enough vision will take three to five years to achieve. A vision that would take more than five years to attain is a sign of an end goal that is too difficult to materialize from a financial and technical standpoint. Also, by the time you build the vision, there is a good chance that the world will have moved on to a new zeitgeist, leaving your effort futile from an economic perspective. However, if a vision can be achieved in less than a year, it is an indication of an unambitious goal that is quite easy to accomplish. It

197

is highly likely that the competition will be able to copy your vision once they see you get traction. They might be able to build better, faster, and more efficiently by avoiding the trials and tribulations that you went through because you already paved the way for them.

A vision should be tailored to your perception of the future and what inspires you within the chosen zeitgeist. Everybody's vision should be unique, but it should be a strong one. That's the characteristic of a good vision. However, there are also many bad ones because it is so easy to do a poor job when it comes to defining a vision. Coming up with a strong vision statement is very hard, but it is imperative to get it right if you want to set yourself up to succeed faster. Before we explore the next level of ideation, it is important to understand what distinguishes a good vision from a bad one.

Strong Vision

Writing a strong vision can solve 50 percent of the problems, but it is a tough nut to crack. A strong vision is an ambitious one with a long-term outlook and is aligned perfectly with the zeitgeist of your era. Most important, it is specific enough to help you execute flawlessly on your business idea.

Let's look at an example of what it looks like to learn how to write good vision statements.

Vision: Build a billion-dollar brand that is admired for helping traditional enterprises innovate the right way by leveraging the power of AI, cloud, and robotics so that they can be more competitive and profitable while doing good for humanity.

Zeitgeist: "AI on Cloud & Robotics to fill the labor gap & declining birth rate."

The vision mentioned here is for my company Techolution for the next five years. In fact, it is a very strong vision. Because I came up with it? Just kidding! Let's break down the vision statement on a point-by-point basis to see what makes it a strong one from a logical and emotional standpoint:

- The vision is very ambitious and long-term enough because it will easily take anyone three to five years to build a billion-dollar brand that is admired for what they do.

- This goal is grand and very inspiring but not impossible to achieve because some people have built billion-dollar businesses in less than five years.

- Most important, the vision is specific enough that we know how we will add value in our field, that is, by delivering technology-based innovation to help clients be more competitive and profitable in today's digital era. There is a big gap in this market currently. Most companies offer IT services, but very few provide outcome-based innovation to enterprises at a fixed price. We do that well and will continue expanding it!

- The market we want to impact is also very well defined: traditional enterprises.

- Last but not the least, this vision significantly contributes to the zeitgeist we want to tap into: AI and robotics to fill the labor gap and declining birth rate in the 2020s. How exactly are they connected? We are helping enterprises innovate with AI, cloud, and robotics so that they can be more profitable and competitive without compromising on the value they deliver to their customers.

Bad Vision

In my experience running a consulting business, I have seen a fair share of enterprise leaders who state that they want to make an impact in a particular field and get on a specific market trend. However, the vision they define for their business does not align well with the megatrend of that period, and sometimes it is entirely different.

Many times, this is an innocent mistake because most people do not follow a systematic top-down approach to set their vision and test its correlation to their zeitgeist. Other times, it is done intentionally because savvy leaders say what the market wants to hear, but they lack the discipline to change the vision for their team to align with what they committed to.

Going from zeitgeist to vision is often where the intentions start to get disconnected from the most efficient path to success. It is crucial to ensure that you don't get your vision wrong if you want to move in the right direction!

Bad visions can be categorized into three types:

1. Disconnected vision

2. Vague vision

3. Weak vision

Knowing what makes your vision bad will help you learn how to create a good vision faster. All three types mentioned here are considered bad. However, they are actually different from one another. To truly understand what to avoid, we need to dive deep and look at examples of what each of these three types of bad vision looks like in real life.

Disconnected Vision

As the name suggests, a disconnected vision is the one where the defined vision statement has no logical and emotional connection with the chosen zeitgeist. It may be formulated without considering the current capabilities, market dynamics, or the evolving needs and expectations of the target customers.

Let's look at an example of a disconnected vision:

Build a billion-dollar brand that is admired for helping traditional enterprises digitize with Salesforce and Enterprise Resource Planning (ERP) software on the cloud so that they can be more competitive and profitable.

Zeitgeist: "AI on Cloud & Robotics to fill the labor gap & shrinking population."

Analysis: This vision is very similar to the strong vision example mentioned earlier. A vision focused on digitizing enterprises with Salesforce and ERP on the cloud may be a good one that could lead to success. However, what makes it bad is that it's disconnected from the chosen zeitgeist: solving a growing problem with the labor gap because of the declining birth rate across the world by leveraging AI on the Cloud and Robotics. We intend to move toward one destination, but the map (the vision) has a different destination plugged in. We may or may not end up somewhere nice, but it will surely not take us where we planned to go in the first place.

Here is a visual representation of a disconnected vision:

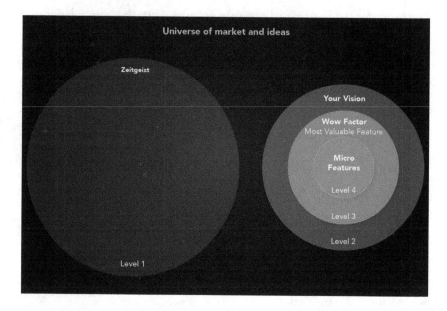

Vague Vision

A vision is vague when the defined statement of the vision lacks specific detail and is only loosely connected with the zeitgeist chosen. In this state, the vision may lack clarity and fail to provide a clear direction or purpose for the organization. It becomes a hazy image that is difficult to grasp and articulate. When a vision is vague, it can lead to confusion, ambiguity, and a lack of motivation among team members.

Let's look at an example of a vague vision:

Build a successful business that helps traditional enterprises innovate so that they can be more competitive and profitable.

Zeitgeist: "AI on Cloud & Robotics to fill the labor gap & declining birth rate."

Analysis: Again, this vision is very similar to the strong and disconnected vision examples above. What makes this one vague is that we want to help enterprises innovate, but we are not specific enough to say how we will do that. The zeitgeist specifically believes that enterprise innovation will happen with AI on the Cloud and Robotics. You can make a claim that falls under the umbrella of innovation. Therefore, being specific on the "how" is very important. For example, developing a cure for cancer is also an innovation. The vagueness of this vision statement makes it loosely connected to the end goal that has to be achieved. It is quite similar to not having any destination plugged into your map but just driving in the general direction of your destination by finding signboards at every turn. This is not a very efficient way to achieve success faster, as you may easily get lost and distracted along the way.

Here is a visual representation of a vague vision:

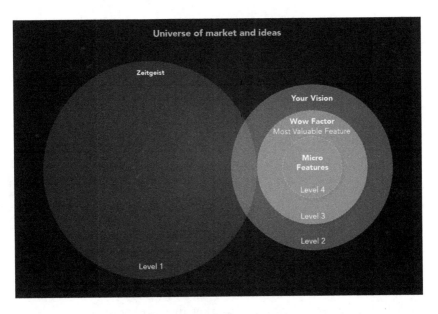

Weak Vision

A vision is considered weak when the defined statement is not ambitious enough and very easy to achieve for the zeitgeist chosen. A weak vision is like setting the bar too low, aiming for goals that are easily attainable without pushing the boundaries or embracing the full potential of the zeitgeist. It lacks ambition and fails to inspire individuals or organizations to strive for greatness and make a significant impact.

Let's look at an example of a vague vision:

Build a cloud-based AI solution that automates the counting of inventory items for retail businesses, that is, grocery stores, and also updates the count in their inventory software in real time.

Zeitgeist: "AI on Cloud & Robotics to fill the labor gap & declining birth rate."

Analysis: This vision statement is very specific and well aligned with the zeitgeist. However, it is considered a weak one because it is actually a feature that might be a potential wow factor. It is relatively easy to achieve and is not ambitious or long-term enough to qualify as a strong vision. This would actually make for a good wow factor candidate that aligns well with the strong vision stated earlier. You cannot tell the difference between the weak vision and the wow factor because they are almost identical.

A few garage-based startups that went on to become very successful businesses started with a weak vision. It was effectively a powerful wow factor, which was well aligned with their zeitgeist. It can be a good way to get started if you are scrappy. However, as soon as your wow factor passes the product market fit stage, you must establish a strong vision that will take your business to the next level in the coming three to five years.

Here is a visual representation of a weak vision:

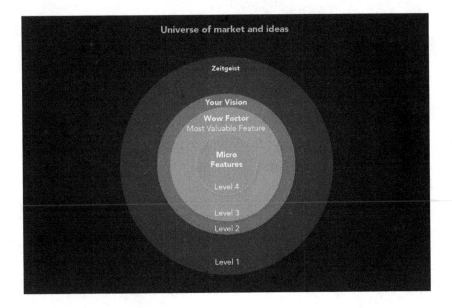

LEVEL 3—WOW FACTOR

A wow factor is not a concept or a grand vision that is achieved over a long period. It is the third level of ideation, a representation of your dream in a form that is tangible and detailed enough to start building your project or business. At the same time, it is articulated in a manner that anyone can understand what value your customers will experience the moment they come in touch with your product or service. It is the unique value proposition of your business that your competitors cannot match in the near future.

A wow factor is the MVF of your product or service offering that will bring so much value to your customers that it will make them say "wow" when they experience it.

This feature could be a groundbreaking technology, an innovative design, or a unique user experience that leaves people amazed and delighted.

As with the example mentioned previously in this chapter, Google launched with only one feature, and they were phenomenal at delivering it to their customers. Their wow factor was "relevant & honest Internet search results in an instant." In the era of Google's formation, all the competitors would flood customers with pages of irrelevant paid listings before a user could find the information they were actually looking for. Internet portals were crowded with information and it consumed a lot more time to find what users needed. Therefore, Google's feature was a definite wow factor for those who were short on time and looking for relevant information on the Internet. It so happened that their wow feature perfectly aligned with the zeitgeist of that period. We were entering the information age with people becoming more connected and mobile, resulting in less patience than ever before in history.

Every business has to have at least one product or service in order to exist. Products and services are made up of one or more features that customers get to experience. However, businesses don't always have a feature that wows their customers. As with the example of Yahoo earlier in this chapter, businesses often start with a wow factor, but over time they lose their focus by growing in various directions and ultimately end up losing their unique value proposition.

Some like Yahoo can last long even without a wow factor based on the brand equity and capital they accumulate in their prime. They failed in spite of being one of the pioneers of the zeitgeist of their time—the Internet revolution. Yahoo teaches us a very good lesson.

Tapping into a megatrend alone is not enough for long-term success. You need a wow factor that aligns tightly with a strong vision and the zeitgeist of your era.

On the other hand, focusing only on your wow factor without evolving with the shifting zeitgeist will surely lead to a rapid demise. This was the story of the famous video rental mega-chain, Blockbuster. They were amazing at cassette and DVD rentals for movies and games when it was in high demand. However, they only focused on keeping their market dominance by continuously sticking to their MVF. In spite of having a strong wow factor, Blockbuster did not evolve fast enough to align with the new zeitgeist: the rapid shift toward on-demand digital movie streaming services in the age of high-speed mobile Internet. By 2010, Netflix was dominating the new zeitgeist, and Blockbuster was forced to file for bankruptcy despite having a great wow factor in its industry.

The lesson that we need to learn from the Yahoo and Blockbuster stories is:

Businesses must be obsessed with their wow factor and its evolution over time, as the competitive landscape and customer

expectations are constantly changing. Do not get complacent, especially when you get really big!

Smart Work Strategy for Wow Factor

To work smart, you must prioritize your battles in their order of importance so that you can go above and beyond in the areas where it will count the most. One of the reasons why we put so much effort into identifying the right wow factor is because it allows us to work smart.

In its essence, the wow factor is like a secret ingredient that sets your product or service apart from the competition, capturing the attention and admiration of your customers. Finding the wow factor puts you on the path of "smart work." It can help you get to your destination by spending minimal resources and in the least amount of time possible. Here's an important rule for working smart when it comes to wow factors: **you MUST go above and beyond to deliver the most amazing quality outcome possible when building your wow factor.**

Every bit of time and money that you put into getting your MVF right to impress your target customers will pay off at least tenfold in the end. It is not practical or feasible to spend plenty of time, energy, and money on every aspect of your business. Therefore, you should reserve it for the wow factor. Even if you had all the time and money in the world, you should not waste your highest level of focus and passion on anything else besides the wow factor.

A good wow factor can take several months to develop, and sometimes it can take even a few years for technically complex and innovative features.

If your MVF is easy to replicate and takes only a few days to develop, then it doesn't qualify as a wow factor. In today's world of cutthroat competition, where technology drives the wheels of change, you need to dedicate a good amount of time to developing your MVF so that you can stay competitive in your industry for the long term. Spending a significant amount of time developing the wow factor allows you to thoroughly assess its market relevance and sustainability. You can conduct thorough market research, gather user feedback, and make necessary adjustments to ensure it aligns with the evolving needs and preferences of your target audience.

DEAL BREAKERS

Since we are on the topic of ideating through features that must be developed so that you can build a viable business to hit the market, it would be a severe negligence if we did not talk about the concept of deal breakers and how it can impact your growth.

Deal breakers are a very important type of feature that is usually captured at the third level of the ideation stage, right after stating your vision. They may or may not directly contribute to your vision or align with your zeitgeist. You might wonder why we should care about this feature at all.

Well, that is because deal breakers are life savers.

Yes, deal breakers are the type of feature that you cannot launch your product or service without. They might not be memorable or solve the core problems that your customers care about all by themselves, but they will ensure that your business stays far away from legal and compliance risks. Their sole purpose is to ensure the survival of your business once the wow factor appeals to your market and you start growing.

For example, the privacy policy for a new website is a deal breaker. If you are building a new website, you would be at major legal risk if you did not have this policy in place. Your customers may never visit this page or appreciate its existence, but you cannot launch your website without it. We call privacy policy a deal breaker because not having one will break your business's existence. Let's learn more about deal breakers by diving deep into Google's example.

In 1998, Google launched their initial product that had only one feature, a search engine platform. It also happened to be their wow factor. Google search had no other features, not even the customary register and login element that all websites had back then. The second-most popular product built by the Google team was Gmail. Its wow factor was "a web-based email system that is fast, accessible anywhere and makes it easier to find the messages you need instantly."

Given the nature of this wow factor, it could not be launched as a product to customers by itself. Emails are very personal in nature, so they must be secured and directed only to the authorized person for ethical, logical, and legal concerns. In fact, the "register and login" feature was a deal breaker that had to be built before the product launch of Gmail when it was introduced in 2004. The login of Gmail had nothing special that other websites didn't already have. It would have been of no value for Google to go above and beyond with it. However, Gmail would not have seen the light of day without this feature. Hence, we call it a deal breaker.

Smart Work Strategy for Deal Breakers

Wow factors exist to impress and delight your customers, so you must go above and beyond. Deal breakers exist for the survival of your business, and they are binary in nature. It either meets the requirement or is not complete. It's a black or white thing with no space for a gray zone. There isn't usually a measure of quality for the deal breaker features. Here's an important rule for working smart when it comes to deal breakers:

You must only do the bare minimum when building and delivering your deal breakers.

Understanding this simple rule will save you a lot of time, energy, and money. It will also save you from the pain of burning out at the execution stage.

A deal breaker usually takes a few weeks, and sometimes a few months, for the more complex ones to develop. Anything that takes longer than three months should be reconsidered or simplified.

Going even a single inch above and beyond the minimum required level with a deal breaker is useless. For example, let's say you need to fill out a form to apply for a government-issued identification, such as a passport. In this case, one of the features you have to consider is the quality of your handwriting. Do you think going above and beyond and taking the time to fill out the form with your best handwriting will change the outcome of your passport's approval? Absolutely not. If you believe in working smart, you should fill out the form with decently legible handwriting as quickly as possible, so you can move on to more valuable activities in your life.

As established previously, every website needs to have a privacy policy. Customers will not visit your website for this policy, and most likely, they will never look at it. However, the law requires you to have this page to launch a website. Do you think going above and beyond and building the most unique or beautiful privacy policy will change what your customers think of the website? Absolutely not! They won't see it, and they won't care. The smart work approach here would be to copy a template from the Internet instead of creating one from scratch. Spend an hour or less customizing it with your name, and then add it to your website so that you can focus all your energy and time on building your wow factor.

Timing Changes Everything

You must make the right decisions about your wow factor and deal breakers today and proceed with confidence. However, remember every wow factor and deal breaker comes with its expiration date.

Timing and context matter when you have to decide on the wow factor and deal breakers. Everything can change over time.

You should reassess the validity of your decisions after every three months. What is a deal breaker today can become a wow factor in another context or time frame. Similarly, what is a wow factor today can become a deal breaker later down the road.

For example, when Google launched Gmail (in 2004) as a web-based email system that was fast, mobile, and easy to use, it was truly a wow factor that disrupted older clunky email systems. As a result, Gmail became very popular and grew quickly. Fast-forward to nineteen years later, all major cloud service providers today offer integrated cloud-based "workspaces" that include email, videoconferencing, chat, and Voice over Internet Protocol (VoIP). All these elements are combined into one web-based system. If Google were to launch Gmail today, it would be viewed as a deal breaker and not a wow factor. Without a cloud-based email, it would not even be able to compete in the cloud-based virtual workspace industry.

This is an example of how a wow factor can turn into a deal breaker over time.

Now, imagine a company that specializes in smartphone manufacturing. In the early 2000s, when smartphones were just emerging, a major deal breaker for consumers was the limited battery life. Many early smartphones struggled to last a full day on a single charge, causing frustration among users.

Fast-forward to the present day, where battery technology has advanced significantly. A company introduces a new smartphone model with a revolutionary battery that can last for several days on a single charge, even with heavy usage. This breakthrough addresses the long-standing deal breaker of limited battery capacity.

Now, this remarkable battery life has become a wow factor for customers. They are impressed and delighted by the extended usage time, as it allows them to rely on their smartphones for longer periods without constantly needing to recharge. The company's innovative approach to battery technology sets its product apart from competitors and generates excitement among consumers. In this example, the deal breaker of limited battery life in early smartphones is transformed into a wow factor with the introduction of a groundbreaking battery technology that significantly extends usage time.

LEVEL 4: MICRO FEATURES

Now that we have explored the first three levels of ideation, it's time to get acquainted with the fourth level, that is, Micro Features (MFs).

These features represent an idea of what needs to be built in the most refined manner. It allows the experts to build, test, and launch smaller end-product components rapidly and frequently. In the popular Agile/SCRUM methodology, the MFs are equivalent to user stories. They help break down the wow factor and deal breakers to a very granular level of detail.

A well-defined micro feature should not take more than a few days to build. In many cases, it is even ready in a few hours.

When you dive deep into this level of ideation, you will come across the Micro Most Valuable Features (MMVFs). They are the most important element of the micro category and originate from your wow factor. On the other hand, those that stem from deal breakers are simply referred to as micro features. It is important to note that these features play a crucial role in enabling modern, more rapid, and iterative agile product development.

At this level, all features must be broken down to a point where they can be fully developed and tested within the typical agile development cycle called sprint. Ideally, this process should take less than two weeks. The hyper-velocity sprints, which I personally prefer, last only about a week. In today's fast-paced environment, all your micro features must be deconstructed to a level where the development takes no more than three days. That gives you two days for testing, fine-tuning, and releasing.

As your business idea moves from conception to execution, the significance of the fourth and final level of ideation becomes apparent. Any errors at this stage can lead to a major hurdle in the development process. Therefore, you must proceed with caution if you want to move faster toward your end goal without wasting a lot of time and resources.

What's Your Wow Factor?

Ultimately, a business can only be as good as the product or service it provides to its customers. Your business will never be great if its core feature fails to evoke a "wow" response from your customers.

Each of the four levels of ideation serves an important purpose at the different stages of the business life cycle to help you avoid the roadblocks and succeed faster in your journey to your end goal. Only after you have identified the zeitgeist of your era should you proceed to refine your most valuable features in a logical order until you find your wow factor and deal breakers. When you make it to the execution stage, you need to break down your wow factors and deal breakers into MMVFs that will provide clear instructions to your execution team members on precisely what to build.

Along the way of this intricate journey, you need to stay focused and disciplined with a methodical test-driven approach in order to make sure that each level of ideation is holistic and can stand strong on its own. Most important, it will help you validate that the idea at each level is highly relevant and correlated to the higher-level idea it stemmed from.

Now that we have established the foundational principles of ideation and wow factors, I am excited to show you how to find your wow factor.

CHAPTER 8 – KEY TAKEAWAYS

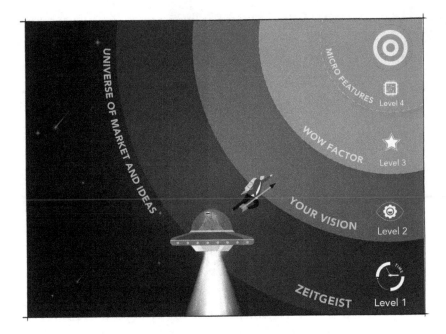

YOUR NOTES

_____
_____
_____
_____
_____
_____
_____
_____
_____
_____
_____
_____

Go Beyond with Your Wow Factor

and do the minimum required with your deal breakers. This is the most important rule to working smart and succeeding faster!

CHAPTER 9

FINDING YOUR WOW FACTOR

The most important secret to succeeding faster at innovation is to find the right wow factor to build for the right day 1 customer, at the right time, in the future when your product goes to market. Therefore,

We must guess the future that we aspire for correctly. The problem is that everything we know is from the past, and everything we think we know about the future is just a guess.

The four levels of ideation that we explored in the previous chapter form a key foundational building block to solving this seemingly impossible problem. At its core, the wow factor is an idea that is represented in the form of a feature. Unlike a regular idea, it should evoke a "wow" response from your customers once they get to experience it.

Many make the mistake of picking a feature that would have "wowed" their customers in the past. So why do people often make this mistake? Well, it happens because the natural decision-making process for most humans is to tap into their existing knowledge base and project it onto the future. They fail to realize that …

Knowledge is an accumulation of information from the past.

Everything that we read and consume is from the past. That is why we tend to make the mistake of solely making decisions based on what we know, the past!

The past can teach us things that will enrich our ability to make better decisions for the future. However, the past cannot predict the future because the future will always be different from the past.

There are others who believe in making decisions in the present. Say the word "present." By the time you are done saying "present," it is already the past! Isn't that fascinating?

What we call the present is actually the immediate past. We should not live in the past because we cannot change it. Therefore, we should not live in the present for it is actually the past. The future is the only place that can be influenced, so let's strive to get it right.

It is much simpler to choose a winning wow factor in hindsight, but if it was so easy to do while looking forward, there would not be as much pain and failure in the innovation and entrepreneurship world. The challenge of figuring out a futuristic winning wow factor is that it must be something your customers will care very much about when you launch it. At the same time, it must be an idea that you feel very passionate about.

In this chapter we will teach you how to find and test your wow factor feature for your day 1 customers based on your future launch date. The first step to finding your wow factor is:

A well-selected zeitgeist followed by a strong vision statement that is future looking, data-driven, and inspiring.

Sounds easy? As you go through the meticulous process of multi-dimensional ideation, it is likely that you will lose focus and come up with a zeitgeist, vision statement, or wow factor that is of high quality and well-meaning by itself but is not strongly connected to each other. It is even more common for leaders to start executing their business idea as soon as they complete a solid market study with a strong vision statement but without having a well-defined wow factor.

Going into the execution mode without finding the *MVF* is the equivalent of flying blind. If the zeitgeist and your vision statement are your destination, then the wow factor is the step-by-step direction that must be followed. It would be foolish, risky, and expensive to embark on a long journey just based on your destination without having your route figured out first. Yet, I see some of the most recognized business leaders make this mistake! Perhaps it is due to overconfidence and faith in their luck.

Most leaders are eloquent at communicating their high-level goals, but when it comes to the executable detail, the majority have no clear plan on how they are going to get there. Some do this intentionally because they need to say the right things to captivate their audience, but they do not have the integrity and discipline to follow through the difficult path of finding a suitable wow factor to execute. However, many make this mistake more innocently because they do not have a proven process to follow. Therefore, they have no choice but to wing it and rely on luck!

Less than 1 percent of leaders have been very successful once based on luck, but even they know that it's not always going to be like that. However, 99 percent of people who go down this journey do not get lucky. Therefore, relying on luck alone is not a viable strategy, especially when there is a repeatable process that can be followed to increase your odds of success.

This brings to mind an example that I witnessed firsthand. This experience taught me how important it is to NOT build any business idea just based on a great vision before finding your wow factor.

Great Vision but Poor Wow Factor: A Case Study

As a young leader responsible for the global e-commerce development of all of Hertz's business units, I witnessed an epic failure of an
established brand genuinely attempting to develop a new product. In
spite of all the firepower that Hertz deployed in launching this new
offering, it was a massive failure because they had an outstanding
vision with no wow factor.

In 2006, Hertz was acquired by one of the biggest private equity
firms in the world, the Carlyle Group. They hired a highly qualified,
visionary, and bold CEO. His job was to transform the company for
the new millennium and take it public. Around this time, the whole
world was changing with the digitization of our lives. As the millenni-
als were entering the workforce, a new trend of urbanization and city
living was reemerging across the United States. The car rental industry
was very old and had an established business model that focused
on professionals (twenty-five years and older) who predominantly
traveled by air and accessed cab services at airports worldwide. This
industry had effectively shunned the highly viable college student
and young professional class who were living in cities by punishing
them with exorbitant surcharges for renting a car. Some car rental
companies would simply not offer their services because of the high
risk of accidents that insurance companies tagged to this market
segment.

Meanwhile, a new startup called Zipcar started to serve a growing
market segment of younger people (aged between eighteen and
twenty-five) living and working in cities that all the established car
rental companies had ignored. It was their wow factor that differenti-
ated them from the established competitors. They leveraged the power

of digital movement to rapidly grow a buzz around this new "local car rental by the hour" model for shorter errands and day trips. Zipcar was the only player serving this market, and it scaled so fast that it became synonymous with the term "car sharing."

My new CEO, being sharp and in touch with the market, recognized this trend and decided to immediately develop a new business unit called Connect by Hertz as an early response to Zipcar's growing popularity. The vision set by our visionary leader was clear and aggressive: to become a market leader with the younger demographics living in cities for hourly car rentals by 2010. While this was a solid vision, I honestly could not articulate to you what our wow factor was going to be, in spite of being deeply involved in the team responsible for building out this new business unit. If I was to name our MVF, it would be to copy everything the competition had already done and try to use our brand power and broader access to capital to grow faster. With a weak wow factor that has no unique value proposition for customers, it is very hard for any business vision to be successful in the long run, regardless of how much funding and executional discipline you have.

I remember being dumbfounded when our legal department put a stop to a very logical initiative I had spearheaded. I assembled a team to develop and promote content digitally that would address the obvious question customers would ask when we launch: "What is the value of Connect by Hertz over Zipcar?" First, our executive leaders struggled to articulate a value proposition other than Connect did what Zipcar did, but it was backed by the giant brand named Hertz. The same company that had shunned the very demographic they were hoping to win now. Second, I was told that legally we were not allowed to go to market with any content or marketing campaigns that would mention or compare us to the competition. In fact, our chief legal counsel told me that we could not even mention the name of our competition anywhere on our website. I found this to be absolutely illogical, and frankly, it exposed the lack of depth and go-to market strategy to accomplish their grand vision.

After blowing through millions of dollars and years of trying to make it work, Hertz had to admit this was an epic failure, and they canned this new business unit. Being a part of this monumental failure taught me some valuable business lessons.

THE LESSON I LEARNED FROM THIS EXPERIENCE

This was the first time I understood that a grand vision is just not enough to succeed fast and win in business. You need to have depth behind the vision with a real wow factor that maps exactly how you will win over the market. Most important,

You should be able to articulate your unique value proposition for the customer without making excuses and hiding behind sophisticated professional opinions produced by savvy intellectuals happy to bill you insanely high consulting fees for their time.

The problem of rushing to execute an idea solely based on a grand vision is not isolated to a few entrepreneurial leaders. It is a systemic challenge prevalent across the majority of the enterprise world. This is why 80 percent of corporate innovation projects fail to complete or deliver their intended value. No wonder CEOs don't stay in their jobs for over five years. This was the conclusion derived from a study done by PricewaterhouseCoopers (PWC) in 2018, which looked at the average tenure of CEOs in the past three decades.[5, 6]

---

5   Peter Gassmann, "Succeeding the long-serving legend in the corner office," PwC, accessed November 20, 2023, Board of Innovation, "Why your innovation experiments fail," accessed November 20, 2023, https://www.boardofinnovation.com/blog/why-your-innovation-experiments-fail/.

6   Board of Innovation, "Why your innovation experiments fail," accessed November 20, 2023, https://www.boardofinnovation.com/blog/why-your-innovation-experiments-fail/.

Many leaders, especially of bigger established enterprises, are really good at coming up with a solid and inspiring vision because of the nature of their job. A strong vision is indeed needed to inspire shareholders, board members, and employees at town halls. However, where the rubber meets the road and the right or wrong turn dictates the success or failure of a business is where most leaders fall short.

Hence, it is imperative to take a top-down approach so that we can bridge the gaps that stall us out when going from vision to the executable wow factor. We start at the highest point and navigate down till we reach a level that contains enough detail to articulate exactly how your offering will give the customer a wow experience when they come in touch with it. This process only works if you resist the temptation and pressure to start building your product until you have a truly meaningful and tested wow factor.

The Five Guiding Principles to Selecting the Right Wow Factor

Resisting the temptation to build a product solely based on a great idea requires a strong commitment to the established process of finding your MVF. It is important to have some guiding principles in place to ensure that you don't deviate from the predefined route. Let's take a moment to internalize the five guiding principles to help you easily navigate the complex path of finding your wow factor.

1. Every wow factor candidate should be treated as a hypothesis.

   As with all hypotheses, it is to be meticulously studied and market-tested until it shows the evidence needed to move forward. It may or may not become the most valuable feature in the future. So do not go on building the first idea you get excited about until you find a wow factor that passes all the tests that you will learn about in this chapter.

2. Be disciplined at not falling in love with your idea just yet!

   Most entrepreneurs and intrapreneurs fall in love with their dream. Falling in love is good because building a startup requires a lot of passion and persistence. Otherwise, if you are open-eyed and rational, you would never take the risk of starting something new and innovative. While it is very hard to be rational when you are influenced by the love for your idea, it requires extreme discipline to not get married to your dream until your wow factor has been battle-tested as an idea. You will need all the love to get through the difficult build phase. So, reserve every ounce of it for if and when you get there.

3. It is difficult to accurately predict a wow factor when looking forward.

   A wow factor is a feature that has the potential to be a winner in your market when it is launched. The benefit of hindsight makes it easy to spot a winning one. However, it is very hard to distinguish between the winner and the losers when predicting wow factors for the future.

4. Do NOT spend any time and money executing your idea.

   You should never spend your time and resources on execution until you have meticulously ensured that the wow factor you want to develop is a winning one. Even if you have expertise in the field, you should not proceed to prototype and proof of concept building. Your time is NOT free, even if nobody is paying you for it right now. You could be distracting yourself from an amazing opportunity that was about to come your way. Therefore, you could be stealing from your own successful future by keeping too busy building mediocre ideas. This rule allows you to make as many pivots as needed at the ideation stage before spending time and money on the most costly part of any project—the development!

5. Apply the right combination of emotion, intuition, and intellectual discipline.

   This one is the ultimate secret sauce to finding your winning wow factor! The best decisions about the future are made with a good combination of emotions, intuition, and a lot of intellectual discipline with test-driven ideation (TDI).

The Nine Steps to Find Your Wow Factor

Now that we have established the foundation by learning the core guiding principles, it is time to explore the step-by-step process that I have developed and tested in the real world for finding wow factors. If you are disciplined in following the process, it will reduce the time needed to find your MVF. It will also significantly lower the pain and cost of getting to your destination. This method cannot guarantee success in finding the winning wow factor of your era, but it will significantly increase the probability of discovering the breakthroughs needed.

We will start with an ideation process that goes through all your raw ideas that can be potential candidates for your wow factor. As you go down this filtering process, we will apply a few tests to ensure that the choices made at each step are good and aligned with the higher-level decisions they stem from when looking forward to the future. By the time you get to the last step of this process, you will have a solid, data-driven wow factor that will be future-worthy and ready for execution.

Let's dive into the nine steps to refine your big idea into an executable wow factor.

STEP 1: FIND THE ZEITGEIST

I strongly recommend that before you start the process of finding your wow factor, first go through the concepts discussed in chapter 7 to find and validate your zeitgeist.

As we learned from the Blockbuster example in the previous chapter, it doesn't matter how great your wow factor is if it doesn't align with the market trends of its time. However, as we previously learned from the Yahoo example, being part of the zeitgeist early enough but not having a relevant wow factor will turn you into a headless chicken, where the death of your business is just a matter of time. Both these factors are equally important, and they are highly connected.

The zeitgeist stands at the highest level of ideation. It is a very broad megatrend that can stay relevant for decades. However, you cannot build a successful business based on a megatrend alone because it is not specific enough to be actionable.

For example, the zeitgeist that we have chosen for my company Techolution is:

"AI on the Cloud & in Robotics to fill the labor gap & declining birth rate."

Time frame of Zeitgeist: 2020–2035

I believe that we are tapping into this megatrend at an early stage. The declining birth rate will lead to a low population count, and the skill gap has been growing across the world since the 2010s. However, it magnified and turned into a new zeitgeist after the COVID pandemic in 2020, when many people worldwide were forced to stay at home. They had time to realize that they didn't need to do unsatisfying jobs or ones that didn't align with their purpose in life.

Since people are being very selective with the work they undertake, it has triggered a global labor shortage, which has been exacerbated by a declining birth rate and retiring baby boomers. This is causing a labor crisis that is leading to unprecedented demand for AI in the workplace to do the mundane manual jobs that people don't want to do anymore. Real-world AI has become a very hot space that will only grow exponentially in the next five to ten years.

Rapidly growing demand alone does not qualify a domain as a zeitgeist. High demand can also be found in Redfield markets, but what makes this a zeitgeist is that the supply of commercial-grade autonomous AI solutions is very limited. AI and robotics is such a difficult field, and the science is still at an early stage. Building autonomous systems to fully substitute the human labor equivalent is a very hard problem to solve. Not many companies have the advanced experience with AI, cloud, and robotics to deliver commercial-grade solutions that businesses badly need in this era.

I chose this zeitgeist for my company from the others because I am very passionate about building autonomous AI systems and super intelligent robots that can do the mundane things we humans don't like to indulge in. The first inspiration for this came at an early age after watching a TV series called *Knight Rider*. I was really inspired by KITT, a high-tech AI-powered automobile that drove the protagonist Michael Knight when he was sleeping on long drives or when he was escaping bad guys in this series (back in the 1980s).

The more practical reason why my company chose to tap into this particular megatrend is because we have gained a competitive advantage in the autonomous AI space as a result of the consulting work we have done for enterprises over the past five years. We have developed expertise and intellectual property that will give us a competitive edge to become a leader in this zeitgeist.

Being clear about the market trend that we will tap into, that is, autonomous AI systems to replace labor shortage, gives us a good high-level direction on where to seek answers. However, it is not specific enough to build anything meaningful. Therefore, we continue with the next steps in this process to refine our idea to an executable level.

STEP 2: AWAKEN YOUR IDEATION MUSCLE

Inertia is a big obstacle for many people when it comes to ideation. It's not that you don't have the ideas and knowledge in you. If your imagination was empty, you wouldn't be here reading this chapter searching for your wow factor.

If you made it this far, then it is somewhere deep inside your head, ready for you to tap into it. The only issue is that your mind has not been opened and trained to tap into all the great knowledge you can access since you don't do this every day.

Let's do a fun exercise to awaken your ideation muscle. It's called creating a 'word cloud,' and it will get great ideas flowing through your mind as water flows down a waterfall.

It is perfectly alright to do this exercise by yourself, or if you prefer, get a few people whom you trust and respect to join you. They could be your friend, business partner, or colleague.

Yes, it is as intuitive as it sounds. You will be creating a cloud of words by following these steps:

1. Close your eyes, and think about the dream that you have been wanting to accomplish. Think about the product or service that you aspire to build.

2. Visualize what it looks like, and also imagine how you would feel when you reach your destination.

3. How would you feel and look when your vision becomes a reality? Just imagine and feel it.

4. Pay attention to whatever flows through your mind and heart. Let it go on for thirty seconds or so, and don't judge it.

a. It's OK if you visualize money, lots of money, happiness from all the luxuries, or the joy of making an impact and helping millions of people whom you care about.

b. Whatever it is that comes to your mind about what will happen when your dream becomes a reality, just let it flow, and please don't judge it. Make sure not to allow anyone in your vicinity who would question your ideas at this stage.

5. Now with your eyes closed, focus your attention on your business itself once your vision for it has been realized.

a. What does it look like?

b. What is it doing?

c. Who are your customers?

d. How do they view your business?

e. How is your business bringing value to customers?

f. What does it do that's unique?

g. What are you proud of?

h. Continue visualizing and feeling more attributes of your business when it achieves the end goal.

6. Now open your eyes, and write the words that represent what crossed your mind as you imagined what your business looks like at its end-goal state.

▫ For example, it could be words like "useful," "big," "admired," "innovative," and so on. Whatever it is, just write on a notepad or type it out.

7. As you scribe each word, how strongly do you feel it represents what your business looks like when your vision is fully developed?

   □ The stronger you feel about the word, the bigger its font size should be expressed on a paper or digital document.

8. Keep on writing words that come to your mind for five to fifteen minutes until your page is full, and it starts to look like a word cloud, with words written in different sizes based on how strongly you feel about it.

   □ In case you don't have enough words to form a word cloud like the one shown in the examples on the next page, it's OK. Don't panic; remember that ideation is a muscle that you haven't been using much. So let's do some reps to build that muscle. Let us go back to step A and start the process again so that you come up with more ideas to add to the word cloud you have started building.

9. At this stage, your word cloud should start to look full. You should have a minimum of ten to a maximum of thirty words on paper or a digital document.

10. Now it's time to pause and re-organize this cloud so that you can see some patterns of common words that have more significant meaning when you think about the future state of business.

11. Copy the words from your initial word cloud to a fresh new paper or digital document with the following guidelines:

   a. The stronger you feel about a given word, the bigger its size should be in writing.

b. For any duplicate word, increase its size on the new paper by one unit, and make it slightly bolder every time it repeats.

c. Place your words on a fresh new sheet of paper or word document such that the words written in the largest fonts end up at the center of the page, and the smaller words are placed around them, forming a layer of circles.

Word Cloud Example

This is a fun warm-up exercise that will get your ideas flowing and give you the momentum needed for the next step. It might also bring to light the words that mean the most to you when it comes to your purpose.

The bigger words at the center of your word cloud may be worth exploring to see if they can lead to your wow factor.

Caution: You should not get carried away by jumping from word cloud to deciding on your wow factor. There is more due diligence to go through before you make that conclusion.

Techolution Word Cloud

The example in the figure above is the word cloud for my company Techolution. After the rigorous due diligence steps, it so happened that the biggest word in our word cloud made it to the center point of our company's vision statement and wow factor definition. It highlighted to us that we were most passionate about "innovation," and that is what we wanted to be known for within our market.

STEP 3: DEFINE A STRONG VISION

Once you pick the megatrend you want to tap into, you need to define your vision, and it should be a strong one. Also, it is very important to evaluate how well it contributes to the zeitgeist it aligns with.

The previous step in this process should have helped you vividly imagine a vision. Now, you need to follow the following sub-steps to define a clear vision statement for your product or service idea:

Sub-Step A: Rewrite your zeitgeist from Step 1.

Chosen Zeitgeist:

Time frame of Zeitgeist:

Sub-Step B: Write the first draft of your vision that significantly contributes to the zeitgeist.

Vision statement version 1:

_____

_____

_____

_____

_____

_____

Sub-Step C: Refer to chapter 8 to assess if the version 1 statement is a strong one.

    i. Does it fit the guidelines of a strong vision?

    ii. If it's a strong one, then proceed to the next sub-step.

    iii. If not, then find out what type of bad vision it is.

    iv. Now adjust your initial vision as per the guidelines of the strong one.

Quick reference of guidelines for strong vision:

a. It directly aligns with and significantly contributes to the zeitgeist you chose.

b. It is ambitious enough that it is not easy for anyone else to copy.

c. It must be achievable so that you can make an impact in a reasonable time frame and cost.

d. It should take at least one and no more than five years to achieve.

e. The progress and end result must be measurable.

Vision statement version 2:

_____

_____

_____

_____

_____

_____

Sub-Step D: Find out how inspired you feel by your vision.

i. Does your vision statement include any of the big font words from your word cloud in Step 2?

ii. If your vision statement above inspires you, then proceed to sub-Step E.

It is extremely important to have a vision that you are very passionate about. You will need all the passion, love, and inspiration to see your way to the finish line. It is just as important to have a vision that inspires you as it is to write a strong one that aligns with your zeitgeist.

So, if your vision statement does not truly inspire you to the point that you get goosebumps when you visualize it, then you have to go back and repeat step 2 to discover a strong one that ignites your passion. Now rewrite your inspiring new vision statement that also follows the strong vision guidelines.

Vision statement version 3:

_____

_____

_____

_____

_____

_____

Sub-Step E: Check whether or not your day 1 supporters feel inspired by this new vision.

Now that you have a strong and inspiring vision that is set up for success, it's time to test it with your day 1 supporters. Everyone embarking on the journey of building a dream should have a few smartly chosen supporters from the start. Ideally, you should test your vision to see if it actually inspires your day 1 customers.

Most of the time, you may not have such easy access to this group of customers, or perhaps you don't feel that your vision is solid enough to run by them. Therefore, it is best that you smartly put together a panel of supporters who are representative of your day 1 customers. You have a lot more access and assistance from these supporters to bounce ideas off at an early stage.

 i. Take your best vision statement so far to your day 1 supporters and get their feedback.

 ii. Are your day 1 supporters equally inspired by the vision you wrote previously?

iii. If yes, then congratulations, you have an amazing vision statement, and you are on the way to figuring out your wow factor in the next step!

iv. If not, then take the feedback and help from your day 1 supporters to rewrite a vision statement that not only inspires you but also them:

Vision statement version 4:

_____

_____

_____

_____

_____

_____

STEP 4: BRAINSTORMING FEATURE-LEVEL IDEAS

Now that you have selected the zeitgeist, awakened your ideation muscle, and articulated an inspiring vision, you are ready to find your wow factor. It will be similar to spotting a needle in a haystack using a finely tuned metal detector.

A. List all the ideas you can think of for the features of your business.

   Listing all the "feature ideas" from your mind to paper is the best way to get started on the journey to find the special one. Once the ideas of potential features start flowing from your mind to paper or keyboard, you will need to triage and take them through a rigorous testing process one at a time until you find the one that passes with flying colors.

B. At this point, don't worry about getting it right or wrong. We are just brainstorming ideas that cross your mind(s) and write it all down on paper, a whiteboard, a spreadsheet, or a Word document.

C. Please don't judge or apply filters at this point because it will stifle the flow. Keep a very open mind, and let the ideas flow from your mind to paper.

D. If you are experiencing a mental block, think about the problem you are looking to solve and what solutions will be helpful. Go back to step 2 to practice the "awaken your ideation muscle" exercise and come back here.

E. If your business idea is in a more established sector (a Redfield market), you can start by listing the key features your competitors offer to their customers.

This will help you establish a baseline of what the other players are doing right or wrong before you can start working on your wow factor.

F. If you do not have in-depth knowledge of the established players in the field you are planning to enter, then go back and research on:

1. Their wow factors,

2. Their deal breakers

3. What do you find significantly lacking with their offering?

4. Most important, what are their customers very unhappy about with their product or services?

5. What are customers commonly complaining about all the existing products or service offerings out there on the market?

6. Write down everything significant that you discover about the competitive landscape in a spreadsheet.

   Now that you have done your in-depth competitive research, write down ideas for wow factors based on the aforementioned steps. Focus on features that can compassionately solve the common problems customers complain about regarding the competition.

G. Repeat the steps from A to E until you have ten to fifty good ideas for features that could be your wow factor.

H. Enter a minimum of ten and a maximum of fifty ideas for wow factors into the "Feature Idea Title" column in a spreadsheet like the one shown here. This is called the wow factor worksheet. Also, for each feature, write down a detailed description of the idea in the "Feature Idea Detail" column so that you do not forget later.

You need to create the following worksheet now, as it will be required to follow the remaining steps in this chapter.

Feature	Feature Idea Title	Feature Idea Detail	Quality-of-Idea Score	Value-to-Customer (0–10)	Value-to-Vustomer Level	Timeliness of Idea (0–2)	Top Down Correlation Score (0–1)	Productivity Score (0–2)
1								
2								
3								
4								
5								
6								
7								
8								
9								
10								

Wow Factor Worksheet

The ideas that you have gathered so far are unfiltered and very likely in a raw format. There are probably going to be very few gems in your list. So it's time to triage this list on your worksheet to eventually get to one idea that is worthy of being called a wow factor.

STEP 5: VALUE-TO-CUSTOMER MAPPING

Value-to-customer mapping is the first of five filtration steps we will cover in this chapter to assess the quality of any idea. It will help you determine how much value these ideas bring to your day 1 customers. It is implied that in order to bring value to the customer, your feature idea must be unique in nature. In other words, it should solve a problem that customers care about that nobody else in the market has yet addressed in a pleasant and scalable manner.

In this step, you have to choose from six very intuitive categories, and there is an associated level of value the idea would bring to your potential buyers. Assign a score between 0 and 10, depending on how much value a feature will bring to your customer, where 0 is the least and 10 is the highest amount of value.

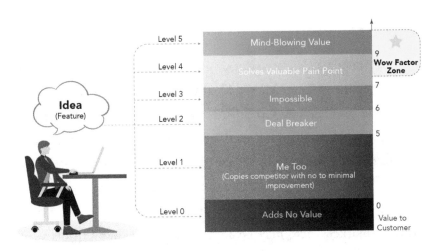

Value-to-Customer Mapping

Level 0: Adds No Value

When ideating, it is normal to come up with worthless ideas before we think of the brilliant ones. While it is part of the journey, it is important to stay objective in the triaging process.

The Level 0 category is for mediocre ideas that would not bring any value to the customer or are completely irrelevant. Being sensitive is not going to be useful in the filtering process.

We need to stay extremely objective and intellectually honest at this stage to find a genuine wow factor. Doing this will pay off big time and save you from immense pain later. If you struggle with being unbiased, seek assistance from others in your network of trusted people who will help you filter the ideas with a realistic mindset.

Scoring: If your idea falls in this category, then assign a value-to-customer score of 0.

Level 1: Me Too

These are features that are very similar to what the other players in the market are offering. Me too ideas stand a small chance of leading to a viable business in a Greenfield market. However, it is worthless in a Redfield or challenging market conditions where the industries tend to consolidate to the few best players. Me too ideas are copycat features of the next best competition and can be a way to build a lifestyle business that may survive in a Greenfield state. In a new growing market, there may be enough room for many to play and benefit. However, you should not expect to make a meaningful impact and achieve any significant success with these copycat features because you will be just another player in a crowded field.

Scoring: If your idea falls in this category, then assign a value-to-customer score between 1 and 5.

Level 2: Deal Breaker

The real value of going through ideas is not so you can impress your customer. "Me too" ideas from competitors can help you understand what features your business needs to have in order to meet compliance, legal and industry norms.

Deal breaker ideas are usually very similar to what the other players have done. There isn't and should not be anything unique and groundbreaking about it. However, they are critical because they will help your business survive. Without developing these essential features, your business may not be allowed to operate, and it even risks being shut down. For more detail about deal breakers, refer to chapter 8.

It is very important to identify features that will not contribute to your success, but without it, your business would not survive. For example, accepting secure credit card payments for any online retail business (in 2023). This feature might not impress your customers. However, without this feature, customers will not be able to purchase from you even if they love your product. Its absence might break your business; hence the name "deal breaker."

Scoring: If your idea falls in this category, then assign a value-to-customer score between 5 and 6.

Level 3: Impossible

This type of idea is way too futuristic, and customers are not ready for it yet. Perhaps the technological advancements needed are difficult to achieve, and there is no established supply chain to help develop this idea in a reasonable budget and time frame. While it may be revolutionary and highly useful to your customer, it is so unlikely to be completed that we assign a lower value.

The case of General Magic that we covered in chapter 3 is a good example of an impossible idea. They were trying to develop the first smartphone in the 1990s, a period when the science, mobile Internet, and supply chain were not mature enough to support their invention. The General Magic group took on this impossible endeavor because they were quite successful and had a huge reserve of capital from their early wins in companies like Apple. While General Magic was not a flop in terms of science and engineering because it set the foundation for the revolutionary iPhone that came a decade later, it was surely a commercial failure!

Impossible ideas are not always bad to pursue, but only take them on if you are genuinely passionate about the impact you think they will make. Most importantly, only follow up on it if you have nothing to lose or you are at a stage in life where you can afford to risk a major financial loss to pursue what you believe in.

Scoring: If your idea falls in this category, then assign a value-to-customer score between 6 and 7.

Level 4: Solves Valuable Pain Point

The ideas in this category genuinely address a valuable pain point for your target market. Your day 1 customers may not be blown away by this feature, but they highly appreciate the fact that you are the first to solve their critical problem. Also, there is no established brand that customers like and appreciate for pleasantly solving this valuable pain point.

These types of feature ideas can be good candidates for your wow factor as long as they are feasible. They may or may not be easy to develop, but they have to be within your reach and realm of possibility. Otherwise, they would be considered impossible (Level 3).

Scoring: If your idea falls in this category, then assign a value-to-customer score between 7 and 9. If the value-to-customer is 8 and above, then it qualifies as a "wow factor"!

But wait, not so fast!

Wow in the Why Test

Just like the popular Test-Driven Development (TDD) framework, we need to apply similar logic to ideas and create a Test Driven Ideation (TDI) concept. This will help us find out whether an idea is really a wow factor before we move forward with the filtering process.

To know whether your idea is truly a wow factor early on, ask why.

A powerful "why" can make people do very extreme things. For example, people go into battles and even give up their lives for the right cause. Innovating and developing a new business idea is no less than going to war. If you want people to give up their time and money to be your early customers, employees, or partners, you need a strong "why." You must have a very good reason that will make them put their lives on hold while they help you make your dream a reality.

Imagine yourself as the leader of a country who wanted to fight a battle with another nation using a purely volunteer army. To do this, you must go around recruiting capable soldiers to join you in the war. The first question they would ask is, "Why should I risk my life by fighting in this war for you?"

If your answer is, "I want to conquer a country and make myself ultra-rich," it's not going to motivate anyone you would want to have in your army. It might appeal to the wrong set of people, who can flee off to another high-paying leader anytime.

But if you were to say, "We need to go to war with the other country because they are planning to launch a nuclear weapon on us that will destroy our nation and potentially our civilization," you've given them a good reason to sacrifice their lives by joining you in this war.

Ask yourself the following three "Why" questions when it comes to developing a feature:

1. Why would my customers be so happy with this feature that they would simply say wow?

2. Why would my customer open their wallets to happily pay me for delivering that feature to them?

3. Why would my customers run and tell others about my valuable wow factor without being asked?

If you cannot answer these questions, either you need to do more research or this idea isn't really the wow factor. You need to downgrade its "value-to-customer" score.

If you don't find your wow factor at this stage, do not settle for one out of impatience. Move to assess the next idea, or simply wait until it comes to you.

Testing your wow factor ideas with your target customers is the first but most important step that will differentiate between success and failure.

For example, I had a customer who wanted to build the next Facebook for fundraising. When I asked him why he wanted to do that, he said, "People right now raise money from Facebook, but it's difficult, and usually there is a social component to it. Usually, it's a fundraiser and people post pictures to kind of make it fun."

I told him: It is a great idea, but may I ask you a few questions about it?

Has this been done already?

How well-known are the competitors with the same idea?

What is the wow factor that differentiates you from the competition?

There are other platforms where you can raise money, and they have the social elements. What is so special about your idea?

The customer stumbled on these questions. They were not able to articulate the pain point they were solving for their market. In fact, they had never even talked to more than one potential customer. This exercise made them rethink their business idea. I was able to save them hundreds of thousands of dollars and months of hard work that would have gone to waste by helping them realize that they needed to scrap the development of this idea until they found a real wow factor.

This client was fully funded and ready to have my consulting firm develop the idea for them. Most of my competitors in the consulting business would have taken their money and built their idea. However, Techolution believes in helping customers with "Innovation done right," so I felt it was my duty to guide them on what I believed was the best way to do it at that time.

There has to be a lot of depth and emotions in the "why" for it to evoke a "wow" response. When you find your wow factor, you will be able to articulate it without stumbling. It will be exciting, and you might even get goosebumps as you explain why this idea is so unique and valuable for your customers.

If you found your wow factor, I am genuinely excited for you. But wait, we still have to do some more critical due diligence at the ideation stage before we start developing anything.

Level 5: Mind-Blowing

You will immediately know when you have a mind-blowing idea. If you have to think hard to assess whether an idea is mind-blowing, then it is most likely not. However, just because you think it is exceptional doesn't mean it belongs in this category.

You need to stay diligent with the TDI process and apply the "wow in the why test" we learnt in the previous section.

Be aware that there are many mind-blowing ideas that really belong in the impossible category (Level 3) and should not be developed unless you are willing to sacrifice a good part of your life to it. Only build impossible ideas if you have an expertise in the domain, you are very passionate about the subject, and you can afford to lose. Therefore, it is very important to dive deeper into mind-blowing ideas to really assess how feasible they are for you to achieve without running out of funds and the time allotted.

An example of a mind-blowing idea for me today is a truly self-driving car. Think of the last time when you were exhausted after a late-evening get-together, but you had no choice than to drive back home. Imagine when you had to drive to work in excruciating traffic, wasting hours of your precious time that you could have spent working on a deadline on your laptop. To me, a self-driving vehicle is a mind-blowing idea, and I would definitely pay for it if there was a truly self-driving car. As much as Elon Musk loves to hype the full-self-driving feature on his Teslas, the reality is there are no such cars in the market today. While Tesla has the best and closest software to self-driving, it is far from being fully autonomous. Although I admire Elon Musk as an innovator, I have to say that he has been falsely advertising this feature (as of 2023).

I find the fully autonomous driving feature to be a mind-blowing one that the world has been waiting for. I have the technical depth in AI and robotics to take on this problem. However, as confident as I am in my ability to solve this challenge, I am well aware that there are several blind spots that I will only see after embarking on this journey. Many tech giants, such as Tesla, Google, and Apple, have attempted to solve this problem for over a decade by spending billions of dollars. Yet, we are a long way from self-driving cars becoming a reality for customers on the road. I am very clear that this is not a wow factor but an impossible idea for me personally at this time. I hope that someone else will launch a true self-driving car by 2030.

Unfortunately, the majority of mind-blowing ideas are actually in the impossible category. However, once in a while, you will stumble across a few gems hiding in plain sight that may be quite achievable, depending on your expertise and network.

Scoring: If your idea falls in this category, then assign a value-to-customer score between 9 and 10.

STEP 6: TIMELINESS-OF-IDEA MAPPING

The value-to-customer mapping process can surely help you eliminate the noise by assessing the practicality of each idea. However, even a great idea can become a flop in a different timeline. Timing is of utmost importance when it comes to succeeding in the business world. You must evaluate the timeliness of your idea by asking yourself this critical question: How unique is your idea in the upcoming time frame?

When you start to develop your idea, the first step should be to figure out whether it's still fresh and hot. Maybe you had a great idea when you were a kid, and now you've grown up and want to make it happen, or perhaps you thought about your business idea three years ago but got really busy and put it on hold. Today, you might be ready and excited to bring your wow factor to the market and kick things off. Before you do this, it is vital to ensure that your idea hasn't expired because, unfortunately,

Every wow factor comes with its expiration date.

What is a wow factor today will become stale at some point in the future, and that is a certainty. If you want to build a highly successful business, you must aspire to find a wow factor that will be appreciated by the market for a long time. This will help you maximize your profits until it becomes obsolete, or the space gets very crowded with competitors. By that time, you should have moved on to your next wow factor that aligns with the zeitgeist of the new era.

It is worth noting that the same rule applies to deal breakers. What was a deal breaker in the past may not be a requirement anymore. In fact, there may be a new set of deal breakers that you may not be aware of that will prevent your business from being viable from a legal standpoint.

For these reasons, any wow factor or deal breaker decision you made over three months ago needs to be reassessed for its validity and re-prioritized based on current market conditions before it gets a green light for development.

For each wow factor identified, assign a score of 0–2 on how unique the idea is going to be at the time you plan on launching it to your customers. This will require you to either surf the Internet extensively or go out in the real world and research what your competitors are doing. You need to focus on both the products/services that are already established on the market and the startups working on similar ideas.

Many people live in their bubbles and are not aware of what's going on out there in the world until they pop their heads out and seek the truth. Most of them will be better off bursting the bubble at the ideation stage rather than experiencing a bigger and more expensive awakening later when they have developed the idea.

You should focus on learning everything important out there about your idea so that you can plan and pivot as early as possible at the ideation stage. To do this, you have to find answers to questions like how unique it really is, what the competitive landscape looks like, if the market is prepared for it, and so on.

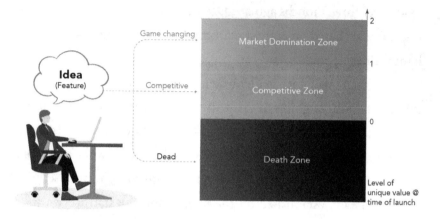

Timeliness-of-Idea Map

After conducting extensive market research over the Internet, talking to customers, and experiencing the competitive offerings, map your wow factor to one of the following three categories.

1. Death Zone

Dead wow factors are wow ideas that solve a problem in an industry that is dying or a market segment that is already obsolete.

Imagine if Blockbuster came back to life (in 2023) with a crowdsourcing model to house DVDs and cassettes in local agents' homes in every town in the United States. You could only order a DVD or cassette from an app, and they would deliver and pick up the movie you rented within one to two hours of placing the request. The price of the movie or game would change depending on the real-time demand. Think of it like an Uber for movies and games on DVDs and cassettes.

This may have been a mind-blowing idea back in 2000 when DVDs and cassettes were popular. I am actually excited to write about this idea. However, the problem is that today nobody uses it. In fact, the Gen Zs would probably say, "What is a DVD?" Almost all movies and games are now fully digital. They are either downloaded or streamed via smart TVs or gaming consoles. Even though the idea by itself is quite unique, it is obsolete and irrelevant in the present time. It does not align with the zeitgeist at all. Such wow factors should be marked as dead and scored accordingly.

Scoring: Assign a timeliness-of-idea score of 0 if it falls in the dead zone category.

2. Competitive Zone

Wow factor ideas that solve a problem in a thriving industry, which has many established and resourceful players, are what we call competitive wow factors. Ideas in this zone should be carefully examined before selection because it takes absolute operational excellence in order for a wow factor idea to break through in a highly competitive market.

As described in chapter 8, the simplistic search engine feature offered by Google (in 1999) was a quintessential competitive wow factor at that time.

Scoring: Assign a "timeliness-of-idea" score of 0.5–1 if your wow factor falls in the competitive zone category, where 0.5 is highly competitive and 1 is moderately competitive.

3. Greenfield Zone

Wow factors that are in a rapidly up-trending market and highly likely to grow your business exponentially to a point where you become a market leader are considered in the Greenfield zone. Ideas in this zone are the best ones to develop. It is important to note that the market must be Greenfield at the time your product is about to launch.

Some good examples of companies that built their legacy on their wow factor in a Greenfield zone are Facebook, Instagram, WhatsApp, Twitter, and LinkedIn. Internet-based social networking platforms were booming between 2005 and 2015. Many players who entered this market with their own wow factors did very well. It's a great example of how multiple players with their unique features can thrive in the same industry in a Greenfield state.

There is a popular saying that comes to mind here: "A rising tide lifts all boats." In our context, it should be: "A rising tide lifts all businesses having a wow factor."

Scoring: Assign a timeliness-of-idea score between 1 and 2 if your wow factor falls in the Greenfield zone at the time your product will be launched.

STEP 7: TOP-DOWN CORRELATION TEST

By now, you should have a few viable wow factor candidates that also score highly on the timeliness test. Before you get too excited and run to develop these valuable ideas, it's important to pause and apply some discipline to the TDI principle we learned earlier. You need to assess how your wow factor is correlated to the vision statement and zeitgeist you previously chose.

Scoring: Assign a score between 0 and 1 on how much you believe your articulated wow factor will help you achieve your vision and tap into its relevant zeitgeist. Be very honest in this assessment, as it will save you tons of time and money.

A top-down correlation score of 0 means that the wow factor may be amazing on its own merit, but it will not contribute toward achieving your defined vision.

A score of 1 (max score) indicates that the defined MVF has a very strong probability of helping you leap toward your vision and tapping into your zeitgeist!

What to do if you have found only one wow factor and it failed the top-down correlation test but has a good value-to-customer and timeliness-of-idea score?

Since it is very difficult to come across wow factors and you have only one so far, you may want to consider pivoting your vision statement and/or your zeitgeist. You need to be careful of "confirmation bias" when re-evaluating your high-end goals before making a decision to change the top-level ideas to match the lower-level gem (wow factor). It is critical to stay objective in this reassessment process because if you make mistakes in judgment at any one of the ideation levels, you will compromise your chances of succeeding fast.

STEP 8: PRODUCTIVITY SCORE

It is hard enough to find one real wow factor, but in the unlikely event you come up with more than one, this assessment will help break the tie and make a decision that will increase your odds of succeeding faster.

Regardless of whether you have one or multiple ideas, go through the list of viable wow factors and assess how difficult it would be to develop. Ask yourself the following three questions:

1. How difficult would it be to build this wow factor?

2. Why hasn't anyone brought this idea to market yet?

3. Do you or your potential team have the necessary expertise to overcome the difficulty and complexity involved in building this feature?

Remember that we are looking for a great unique feature that would make the customer go wow. We are not aiming for every little detail to be taken care of to perfection on day one because,

Perfection is the enemy of productivity and profitability.

It's about choosing the right battles to take on at the right time. If you're getting distracted with battles that won't help you win the war, then you're just going to run out of energy, money, and people. This will ultimately lead to a massive failure.

Replace the idea of perfection with "great and productive."

Scoring: In the spirit of focusing on great and productive, give each wow factor idea a productivity score between 0 and 2.

A productivity score of 0 would be assigned if the wow factor is very challenging to build and your team doesn't have the required skills or experience to solve such a problem.

On the contrary, you give it a productivity score between 1 and 2 if this is your area of expertise. You should be confident in your ability to put together a team of people with the right skill set to build this wow factor by leveraging your past experience in this space.

STEP 9: QUALITY-OF-IDEA SCORE

The Quality of Idea is an ensemble filtering technique that combines the last four evaluation criteria to provide a singular meaningful score. When put together in a weighted formula, as shown next, it gives us a single source of truth that represents the idea's quality.

Quality-of-idea score = Value-to-customer score × Timeliness-of-idea score × Productivity score × Top-down correlation score

Let's review the four filtering scores that make up the equation for the quality-of-idea score:

1. Value-to-Customer—Step 5: Score between 0 and 10

2. Timeliness of Idea—Step 6: Score between 0 and 2

3. Top-Down Correlation—Step 7: Score between 0 and 1

4. Productivity—Step 8: Score between 0 and 2

Selection Rules

Let's take a look at the final selection rules for your wow factor ideas:

A. As you go through steps 5–8, you need to enter the respective scores one by one for each idea on your list in the wow factor worksheet. Set up the quality-of-idea column with the equation shown previously so that it automatically computes the quality-of-idea score as you enter the values in steps 5–8.

B. The quality-of-idea score for each wow factor can be 0 at minimum and 40 at maximum.

C. Use the quality-of-idea score to sort through your feature-level ideas where you select the wow factor with the highest value as the winning one.

D. Any feature idea with a quality-of-idea score of 0 is disqualified, and anything with a value-to-customer score below 8 cannot be considered as a wow factor to begin with!

The Way Forward

Now that we have completed the internal testing, we must take our most qualified wow factor to our day 1 customers. At this stage, it is critical to run your chosen wow factor by your target customers to validate whether they naturally react with a "wow" upon hearing your concept. The TDI process dictates that you carefully listen to your day 1 customers as early as possible and objectively analyze their organic feedback to validate your idea, evolve it, or completely pivot at the ideation stage before embarking on the expensive build phase.

With a wow factor in our arsenal, it is time to learn the next most important success factor—how to choose the right day 1 customer.

CHAPTER 9 – KEY TAKEAWAYS

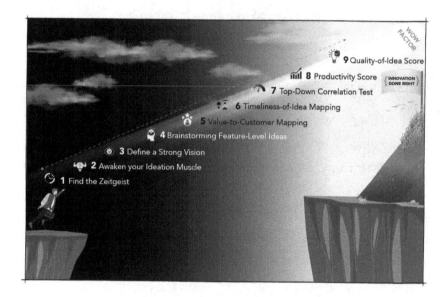

YOUR NOTES

_____

_____

_____

_____

_____

_____

_____

_____

_____

_____

_____

_____

_____

_____

Succeed Faster **SECRET #8**

Choose the Right Day 1 Customer

The right day 1 customer will scale the awareness of your wow factor fast and far enough to spiral your business to a viral level of growth.

CHAPTER 10

THE VIRAL SPIRAL CUSTOMER

t is common knowledge that no business can survive without customers. The more successful a business is, the more consumers they must have. Investors have traditionally valued businesses on revenue growth and profitability. Recently, Venture Capitalist (VC) firms disrupted this long-standing conventional wisdom of the professional investment industry.

In the late 1990s, the VCs decided to scrap the revenue and profit metrics in exchange for hype and hope as a measure of success for the companies they invested in. I am not sure exactly how they measured these metrics to pick the winners from the losers. Eventually, the laws of finance prevailed as this strategy blew up on them when the dot-com bubble burst in 2000, sending the entire economy into a recession. Many investors lost their wealth overnight when tech startups like Pets.com went from being the latest Silicon Valley unicorn to worthless in a matter of days.

Logic would have it that the VCs would learn their lesson from this epic failure and revert to conservative investment principles that have withstood the test of time. Being the champions of business innovation that they are, the VCs came back with a vengeance in 2004. In this round, they invested even more in unprofitable startups with no revenue, such as Google and Facebook, because these companies were offering their services for free.

However, this time it was truly different! The VCs learned from their past mistakes and evolved their investment thesis to a disruptive and brilliant new strategy. They measured the virality of the business idea. In other words, they analyzed how likely the business idea is to go viral and achieve exponential customer growth in the near future. Their calculus was that rapid customer growth (virality) is the best early-stage predictor of future profitability. The VCs pushed the boundaries by demanding their companies to forgo near-term profits and go all in with their capital deployed toward rapid customer acquisition growth. In the end, this strategy paid off in a big way. Many VCs and startup founders became billionaires in the past two decades for incubating some of the greatest companies of modern times: Amazon, Google, and Facebook/Meta, to name a few.

As an investor, it is easy to search for businesses that already have significant momentum with customer growth. This can be forecasted with simple analytics. Trend the historical data on a chart, and make reasonable projections about their future. However, innovative ideas do not have the luxury of data at the ideation stage, making it difficult for business leaders to predict the virality of their idea before going to market. In this context, the billion-dollar question for startup founders and enterprise leaders is,

What is the best predictor of the future virality of a business at the ideation stage?

It is the Wow Factor and the Right Day 1 Customer! These are the two most meaningful early-stage predictors of whether a new business idea has the potential to go viral in the future after it is built and brought to market, resulting in major success for the leaders and investors who incubated the innovative concept.

In the previous two chapters, we learned what a wow factor is, how to find it, and its importance in succeeding faster with a new business idea. If the wow factor is like a marvelous new rocket ship, then the day 1 customer is the fuel that will propel the rocket ship toward escape velocity in space, far away from the earth's heavy gravitational pull.

Failure is like gravity. It is the natural state of things in life. You have to do nothing to fall and fail, but you need to do many things right to take off and keep on flying high to your destination.

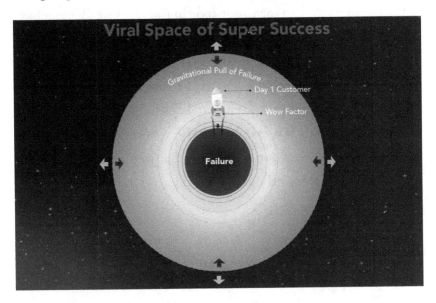

Escaping the Gravitational Pull of Failure

Given the fact that you do not have to do much to fail in this world, it puzzles me why so many people in the business arena are making it their goal to fail fast and fail often. Do nothing, and you are guaranteed to fail very fast. The most effective way to escape the gravitational pull of failure in business is to first get your wow factor right. The ideal wow factor can take you through the first 50 percent of the journey toward success. While this progress is much better than zero, it still falls in the realm of failure. Getting your day 1 customer right will help you cover the remaining 50 percent of the journey toward your destination.

Wow factors are hard to find and often very challenging to build. So, it is natural to wonder whether you can just skip them and go straight to the day 1 customer with a "me too" or mediocre product offering. Unfortunately, there are no shortcuts to achieving anything great in life. You should consider finding and building your wow factor as the rite of passage to earn your spot in the League of Champions. From a more practical perspective, your day 1 customer will probably not buy your product/service without a wow factor. Even if they find some value, they might not be excited enough to spread the word about your offering to their friends and family.

If you want to fail fast, go to the market with your day 1 customer alone. But if you want to go far, you need to have both the right wow factor and day 1 customer by your side.

THE RIGHT DAY 1 CUSTOMER

Not all day 1 customers are equal! Some of them are good, while others can be bad for your business. This is why it's so important to choose your day 1 customer very carefully. Let's find out how the good and the bad day 1 customer can influence your business growth.

There was an amazing new pizza restaurant that had just opened at the end of a quiet alley in the Dumbo district of Brooklyn, New York. They make the best pizza ever. It's really good and very different from all the other pizzas out there. Everybody who has ever tried this pizza falls in love at first bite. "Wow" is the first word that comes out of people's mouths after they take the first bite into their slice. This is a full-service sit-down restaurant with a nice ambiance. They also serve drinks, coffee, pasta, and dessert. People enjoy the ambiance and often order drinks and desserts, just like they do at other restaurants across the city. Nonetheless, the pizza is the only reason why people come to this restaurant again and again. Nobody says "wow" for anything but the pizza. It's clearly a wow factor for this restaurant.

Now, let's take a scenario where nobody knows about this amazing restaurant because the owners were only focused on making great food but were terrible at getting the word out to spread awareness of their delicious new pizza. Joe was their day 1 customer. He lived a block away and was the first one to stumble upon this place on their opening day while jogging down the quiet alley where nobody goes. Joe visited this place to give their new pizza a try and fell in love at first bite. A week later, he brought some of his best friends to share a piece of this deliciousness. Joe and his besties agreed not to tell anyone else about this awesome pizza place because they didn't want to ruin their experience by making it famous. They didn't want to wait in line for an hour like they had to at other famous restaurants in the city.

Six months go by, and Joe and his besties are still the only customers of the best pizza place in the world. They come here three times a week for lunch. One cold Saturday afternoon, Joe went downstairs and stepped out of his building. He looked at all sides to make sure nobody was following him to his secret pizza place. He was very hungry, so he walked fast down the alley. His mouth was watering as he approached the storefront. Joe's excitement abruptly turned into panic when he arrived at the front door. He pulled on the door handle, but it would not open. He tried harder a few more times until he realized the doors were locked. He looked inside and immediately noticed that the lights were turned off. He then turned to the side window and saw a big red "For Sale" board taped to it. Joe yelled, "What the F*" as he realized what had actually happened. In spite of being the best pizza in the world and having a clear wow factor, this business had to close down forever! As Joe calmed down, he was reflecting on how this could happen.

If I were there with Joe at that time, I would have told him that this happened because they had the wrong day 1 customer. Joe is the worst possible day 1 customer any business could wish for.

Now let's consider an alternative scenario where instead of Joe, they had Jane as their day 1 customer. Jane is a nineteen-year-old college student who lives in the same building as Joe. Jane works as a local tourist guide for one of the popular New York City tour buses during the day, and she attends classes at her local university in the evening. She discovered this pizza restaurant on the first day it opened while strolling around her neighborhood on her day off. After giving their delicious pizza a try, she fell in love at first bite. The next day, Jane brought five of her friends after her evening class to try this new restaurant. All five of them had the same reaction: "Wow!" Each one of her friends brought five other people for dinner at this place in the days to follow. Within a week, word spread at their college that the best pizza in town is around the corner. Two weeks after her first visit, Jane comes back for a late-night pizza dinner. She was happy to see the place she just discovered was packed with her college crowd, and she did not mind waiting for fifteen minutes to be seated.

Jane was just as delighted with the pizza as she was the first time. With the validation of the larger crowd at the restaurant, she felt confident to share it with the tourists on her tour bus the next day. Jane told them, "The best-kept secret of New York City is down this empty alley right here." The next day, as her tour bus was passing by the alley, she noticed that something had changed. There was a long line outside of the pizza place, and you could see all the people waiting down the alley from the main street. She grabbed the microphone and proudly announced to her new group of tourists on the bus, "You see that long line there, I was the first one to discover this place! These are college students and tourists waiting for a slice of the best pizza in the world." By the end of the week, the line backed up all the way to the big crossroad. Anyone passing by the main street could notice the crowd without even looking down the alley. Before you know it, every tourist guide in New York was telling their passengers about it on their tour buses. All the working people who lived in the vicinity were annoyed and curious about why their quiet residential neighborhood was suddenly attracting so much attention.

Martha, a resident in the same neighborhood, is an editor for a world-renowned magazine based out of New York City. Like others, she was curious after seeing the crowd on her walk back from work in the evening. The very next evening, she stood in line to see what this buzz was all about. After standing there for an hour, when she got to the counter in the restaurant, Martha said, "Give me what everybody else is ordering." The man at the counter smiled and responded, "That would be ten dollars, please." She was shocked at the idea of paying $10 for a single slice of pizza because every other place charges $5 at most. Since Martha was here on a mission, she didn't object and handed her credit card to the man at the billing counter. She could not wait to uncover the reason behind their audacious pricing, charging over double what other pizza restaurants do for a slice.

Five minutes later, a kind gentleman came to her table and served what she believed to be the most expensive slice of pizza in the world. She took her first bite, and the magic kicked in. It was another case of love at first bite. Martha could not help but react the same way as everyone else who lined up there. "Wow," she screamed! One month later, she wrote an article in her world-renowned magazine about "A Slice of Wow in New York." At this point, millions of people worldwide who read this magazine became aware of the little pizza place that opened just two months ago.

Jane became upset at herself for helping make this place famous because now she had to either wait in line for two hours or make a month-long advance reservation to eat there. She continued stewing about how unfair karma was to her. She was kind enough to spread the word about a new restaurant for free, and now she couldn't practically go back there to eat without wasting half a day. To make things worse, her peaceful residential neighborhood had become another crowded tourist spot in the city.

It just turned midnight, and Jane could not sleep because she was fuming about this unfair situation. She looked out of her window and saw the alley was quiet. The restaurant owner approached the storefront from the inside to lock the front door as the last customer of the day was walking out. With all these thoughts of indignation in the back of her mind, Jane stormed down to the restaurant and knocked on their door. The owner walked to the door from the inside to tell her the restaurant was closed. She yelled, "I don't want your pizza. I just want to tell you that I was your first customer who spread the word to all my university friends and passengers on the tour bus about how amazing your pizza was when nobody knew about this place. I did it out of kindness and for free. Now I have to wait for two hours just to buy a slice of what used to be the best pizza." The owner remembered Jane and felt bad about what had happened. He opened the door and thanked her for everything she had done. He handed his business card to Jane and told her, "My personal mobile number is on the card. Anytime you want to eat here, just send me a text message, and I will personally give you VIP access from the back door that is only for staff." Jane felt so relieved as her anger melted into gratitude. She thanked him and walked away. The owner called her back to say, "Oh, one more thing. Your next meal here is on me."

The moral of the Joe and Jane pizza story is:

Only the right day 1 customer will spread the awareness of your wow factor far enough to spiral your business to a viral level of growth.

The Most Popular Day 1 Customer

The most popular day 1 customer is "everybody." We all wish for everyone on the planet to become a customer of our business on day 1. You will go down in history as one of the most successful startups ever if you can make everyone out there a happy customer on the first day of launching your business.

Many established enterprises and startups reach out to my consulting firm, Techolution, to help them build their next great business idea. The first question I ask them is, "Who are you building this product for?" The most common answer that I get is everybody. My standard response is, "That's great. I like your ambitions, and I hope that eventually everybody on the planet will be your customer." Then I ask them the question again a little differently: "On day 1, when you go to market, who is the customer you are building your product for?" At this point, most people usually look at me with frustration, wondering why I am asking them the same question twice. They usually respond with an angry tone: "As I told you, we want to build a product for everybody. Just like Google, Facebook, and Stripe, etc. We don't want to discriminate; we want to serve everybody on day 1."

This time, I can't help but transgress into lecturing mode. I have to explain to my ambitious clients that the mega-successful modern businesses that they are inspired by did not target their product to everybody on day 1 when they went to market. They did not even intend to be as successful as they ended up becoming. For example, Google was trying to make a search engine that was fast and accurate for college students at Stanford University on day 1. Similarly, Facebook was focusing on connecting "friends" on the Harvard University campus. In fact, their first version only allowed access to users who had a Harvard email address. In the early stages, Tesla was only trying to build a car that would appeal to a very tiny demographic living in California's Bay Area. They were targeting people who loved and could afford fast cars and also strongly believed in helping the planet become greener.

This brings to mind one of the most important laws of marketing: "When you try to appeal to everyone, you appeal to no one."

Similarly, I have discovered the first law of virality:

When you try to wow everyone, no one comes. When you wow the right first customer, then everyone follows.

The Path to Virality

The day 1 customer can make or break you in the first go-to-market phase of your business. Choosing the right day 1 customer holds the key to getting you through the first out of three waves of exponential customer acquisition growth, which can make you go viral.

The path to virality is never a straight line. After you go to the market with your wow factor, rapid customer acquisition growth happens in waves until it spirals out of your control to hit escape velocity and enter the viral zone.

Once a business achieves virality, it enters what we call the viral space. Let's learn more about the three waves that make up the spiral path to virality:

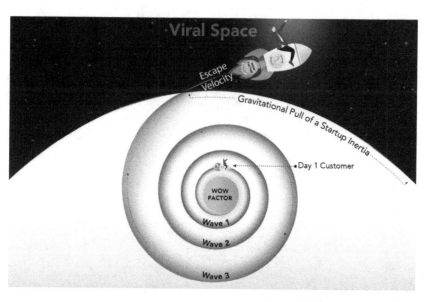

The Spiral Path to Virality

WAVE 1

The first wave of exponential growth is led by your day 1 customer. Once you build your wow factor for the right day 1 customer, you let them experience it. They fall in love with your wow factor and voluntarily share it with others in their immediate circle without you asking them to do so. It could be friends, family, neighbors, or a group that they are part of. They would usually tell people in their circle who share the same problem that your wow factor solves for them.

At this stage, the awareness of your wow factor is spreading rapidly without you spending any money on marketing. Simply because your day 1 customer loved what you offered and is spreading the word out, just like Jane did in the pizza restaurant story. If you recall from earlier in this chapter, Jane brought five of her college friends to the pizza place that she discovered for dinner. Also, in the next few days, she spread the word to all the tourists on her bus that it was the best pizza in the world.

As we learned from Jane's example, the right day 1 customer is the one who gets your first wave of exponential growth going.

WAVE 2

The waves of exponential customer acquisition growth move in sequential order. Wave 1 has to happen first before wave 2 can take place. In fact, the first one leads to the second.

During wave 2, the awareness of your wow factor spreads to people who are three to five degrees of separation away from your day 1 customer. Your day 1 customers told their friends about your wow factor in wave 1. Now their friends are telling other people about your wow factor. Iteratively, the word is spiraling to the next layer of people.

In the Jane story earlier, wave 2 starts when each of her five friends brings five others in the next few days of eating that delicious pizza. The new group of friends tell other friends, and before you know it, many friends of friends of friends at her university are lining up for the pizza. Other tourist guides, who had no connection to Jane, noticed the line outside the pizza shop and informed the tourists on their tour buses about it, ultimately contributing to the second wave. The most important event that led to wave 3 was completely outside of the control of the pizza shop owner or the day 1 customer, Jane. It happened when Martha, the editor of a popular magazine, got curious about the long lines forming near the building where she resides.

Those who focus on maintaining a consistent wow experience of their product to all the new customers lining up end up progressing to the next big wave of growth. Scaling consistently at this pace of growth is not easy, and many businesses begin regressing in the quality of their wow factor or their customer service experience. At this stage, the best practice is to prepare your operational team and processes to scale for wave 2 as soon as wave 1 begins spiraling to the next level.

WAVE 3

Wave 3 is the final wave of growth on the path to virality. At this stage, the exponential growth curve gets steeper by the day as the word about your wow factor has completely spiraled outside of your control. You lose the ability to personally connect the dots of how all the new customers are finding out about your wow factor.

At some point in this wave, the media and social network influencers cannot help but notice the buzz your wow factor is creating. Since their large audience expects them to cover trends, they feel compelled to give your business a high level of exposure for free. Most startups would not be able to afford this level of exposure in equivalent paid advertisement. In the Jane story, wave 3 gained momentum when Martha wrote about the "wow" pizza in her world-famous magazine. Her action helped the pizza restaurant achieve escape velocity, and now everyone wanted to experience the "wow" pizza. This event triggered other media outlets and influencers to give them more exposure, and now everyone wants to follow. Once they entered the viral space, customers were willing to wait in line for two hours and book a table one month in advance.

Wave 3 holds a lot of power, and with great power comes great responsibility. This final wave can either propel you to great heights or leave you in a worse situation than ever before. Let's take a deeper look at the two possible outcomes of wave 3.

A. Wave 3 Is Extremely Rewarding

Assuming you are able to scale your execution to maintain a consistent wow factor quality and customer service despite the steep and sudden exponential growth of your customer base, then you will have attained the escape velocity needed to achieve virality! The viral space is a league of champions where everyone follows your day 1 customers and lines up to experience your wow factor.

In viral space, businesses normally become too big to grow exponentially because everyone is already a customer. There are ways to maintain healthy growth at this stage by upselling and cross-selling. Before we digress too far beyond the path to virality, let's table the topic of growth in the viral space for another book!

B. Wave 3 Damages You

In wave 3, whether you intend to or not, you and your business will get a lot of exposure from people you know and even from those who you don't know. At this stage, everyone is getting interested in doing business with you. Your wow factor becomes a celebrity all of a sudden. It is extremely difficult to scale your business operations and keep up with this rapid increase in demand for your offering. Preparing for wave 3 before it actually kicks into action is too expensive and premature. That is because you will need a different set of people, skills, tools, and processes to scale successfully at this level. In the next section of this book, we will explore a model for executional excellence that works at this level.

With all this attention on your business, if you are unable to maintain a consistent wow factor and customer service, your reputation will take a hit. It may become impossible to recover and get a second chance with a severely damaged reputation.

In the story told earlier, Jane was initially eager to spread the word about the new pizza restaurant she discovered on day 1. Now that the business was in wave 3, she became very dissatisfied with their customer service. She felt that the insane wait time and the long lines outside of her building were not how she deserved to be treated for her early contribution. Jane was very upset, and she would have likely gone out of her way to inform the new tourists on her tour bus that this pizza restaurant is highly overrated and expensive. She could go and spread negative sentiments about this place in her university. Fortunately, the owner had the wisdom and empathy to appease Jane, so she was no longer motivated to damage his business reputation.

Eight Steps to Choose the Right Day 1 Customer

In the previous chapter, we looked at the nine steps to finding your wow factor. In the process of test-driven ideation, the first nine steps help us with brainstorming, filtering, and internally testing our wow factor ideas. The next requirement is to do a "Day 1 Customer Test."

Just because we think a feature idea is a wow factor and it passes all of our internal tests, it does not mean that it will actually be a wow factor for our day 1 customer. At this point, our wow factor idea is properly formulated, and we know exactly what problem we are solving with our business idea. Now it is time to street test it with our day 1 customer. By the end of this process, we need to be clear on who we are solving for when we go to market on day one.

Let's get into the eight steps to choose the right day 1 customer:

STEP 1: TOTAL ADDRESSABLE MARKET VALIDATION

The total addressable market (TAM) is the measure of the size of the entire market that you may be able to serve if and when your business idea achieves complete virality. It translates to the maximum number of consumers you will end up acquiring years down the road once everyone who cares about the problem you are solving becomes a customer. TAM is the total market you can possibly address, assuming there are no competitors you need to split market share with.

For example, the TAM for a pizza restaurant in New York City would be equal to the yearly average of the total residents and tourists in the city who may be interested in eating pizza. In this case, small children without teeth would not be able to eat pizza; hence, they cannot be counted as part of the TAM. Therefore, you cannot simply look at the total population from the census data. The entire population of the city, plus the tourists and minus the babies, is the TAM for our wow pizza restaurant idea.

The TAM metric only gives you an idea of the potential future demand. If you pick your zeitgeist carefully, then you can safely assume that the TAM of your market will be big enough. It only looks at the demand variable and does not consider supply. The relationship between those two variables is closely analyzed when selecting a zeitgeist.

The reason why it's important to evaluate the TAM is because the zeitgeist study was based on a high-level industry trend. When we were looking into the zeitgeist, we did not have our feature-level detail figured out. Now that we know exactly what our wow factor is, we need to check if the TAM (in the context of our wow factor) is big enough to be financially viable. That is because your feature idea can genuinely be a wow factor, but it may only be applicable to a very small group of people worldwide. In such a case, it likely won't be commercially viable as there may not be enough paying customers to serve. We need to complete our due diligence to ensure that there is enough potential in the market before spending the next several years taking major risks and working very hard.

Normally, we want to make sure the TAM of the market we are targeting is very large. Ideally, the number should be in billions or, at the very least, in millions. The only scenario where a small TAM is worth pursuing is when our wow factor is dealing with high-value transactions accompanied by high profit margins.

Let's say you were granted a patent for inventing a device that would make all the existing nuclear power plants in the world three times more efficient and ten times safer than they currently are. On average, it would increase the profitability of each nuclear plant by $100 million per year. Since your patent gives you a monopoly on this market for the next twenty years, you could charge each nuclear plant $50 million for your device, allowing them to still net a solid profit increase of $50 million. There are only 430 nuclear power plants in the world. Your TAM of 430 appears to be a very small market at first sight. However, when you multiply 430 by the transaction value of $50 million per nuclear plant, that gives you a TAM of $21.5 billion that you can go after without any competition to worry about!

Enter the dollar value of your TAM in the fifth column in the spreadsheet, as shown in the figure below.

Day 1 Customer Virality Assessment

Wow Factor #	Wow Factor Title	Wow Factor Description	Quality-of-Idea Score	TAM in Dollars
1				
2				
3				

Total Addressable Market (TAM) Value for Wow Factors

What is the TAM (in dollars) for your wow factor?

If this TAM value is too low, do not proceed to the next step. Move on to assess another wow factor!

STEP 2: DAY 1 CUSTOMER GROUP SELECTION

When we say day 1 customer, we are not necessarily referring to a specific person. It is actually a group of people who share a particular type of persona. They usually have the following in common: demographics, geographical area, a strong passion for the specific problem we are solving, and members of a profession, institution, and/or club.

For example, the right day 1 customer in our pizza story could have been Tina instead of Jane. Tina is Jane's friend at her college, and they live in the same building. Tina enjoys eating pizza for dinner once a week, and she also has a part-time job as a New York tourist guide for a competing tour bus company. In fact, it could have been anyone else who met the criteria of what we can call the "Jane" persona.

List one to three groups that you believe would be good candidates for day 1 customers to go to market with your wow factor. For each group, define up to five criteria that their persona has in common. Use the form shown in the following figure to complete this step:

Day 1 Customer Group Candidates

Group #	1	2	3
Group Name			
Group Description			

Persona Criteria

Geographic Location (Neighborhood preferred city is OK or state max)			
Age Group (1-15 year gap max)			
Profession (Be as specific as possible)			
Institution or Club (Be as specific as possible)			
Optional Criteria #5			

Day 1 Customer Group Candidates Form

STEP 3: NETWORKING STRENGTH SCORE

The networking strength score measures how connected and influential are the people in a particular group. This step is perhaps the most critical one in differentiating between the right and wrong day 1 customer. This test would have helped us identify early on that Joe was the wrong day 1 customer and Jane was the right one.

The network strength is measured by the following:

1. How big is the network of this group?

2. How social is the group?

3. Do they have a platform where they can influence people?

4. How many people are they able to influence at a time?

5. How likely are they to share information with one another voluntarily?

6. Do they share information in person or digitally?

7. How active are they on social media?

8. How actively do they participate in face-to-face events?

9. How do others respond to them on social media?

10. How friendly is this group of people?

Scoring: Enter a score between 0 and 2 that signifies the networking strength of this group. Please note that decimal point scores are permitted here.

For each group you listed in step 2, assess the strength of their network.

For example, in the pizza story earlier, I would have given Joe a score of 0 for network strength because he has only three close friends whom he socializes with. He is also quite private and does not like to share things with outsiders or on social media.

On the other hand, I would give Jane a network strength score of 1 as she has many friends in college who she frequently meets and shares things with. Jane is a very social and friendly person. Most importantly, she works as a tourist guide and has the ability to influence over fifty tourists (daily) who are on a mission to explore the city and spend money on local experiences. Jane has the attention and respect of this group because they rely on her for guidance on what to do and where to eat in the city.

Martha, the editor of the world-famous magazine, would get a full score of 2, as she has an influence on millions of people who could be potential customers of the pizza restaurant.

STEP 4: NAME YOUR DAY 1 CUSTOMERS

If you are an introvert with an analytical mind, then you have probably been in your comfort zone so far. We have gotten pretty far in our journey without speaking to any real people. Now is the time to put your extrovert hat on or find a friend who is not shy to speak to strangers. Let's go interview our actual day 1 customer candidates one by one.

First, let's identify three to five names of people who are part of your day 1 customer group. These are individuals who fit the persona of the groups you identified in step 2.

Group # _____

Group Name _____

Day 1 Customer Group Persons

Person #	Person Name	Passion for Wow Factor Score (0-10)	Affordability Score (0-1)	Reachability Score (0-1)	Contact Info
1					
2					
3					
4					
5					
	Average Scores				

Name Your Day 1 Customer Group People

In the next two steps, you will have to speak to the people you have named here (in person) to validate if they are the right customer group. As shown in the figure above, you will individually score their passion for the wow factor. These individual values will be used to compute an average score for the entire group in the following respective steps.

STEP 5: PASSION FOR WOW FACTOR SCORE

Meet your day 1 customer (on the list in step 4) one by one and tell them, "I am working on solving a business problem, and I would be grateful to have two minutes of your time to tell me what you think."

Go on to articulate your wow factor, and explain how it works without selling or preaching them. Keep the conversation focused on what the wow factor does.

This exercise must be done in person, and you need to be able to observe their body language and their facial expressions.

Find out their natural reaction when you are telling them about your wow factor.

Scoring: Enter a score of 0–10 on how passionately the person reacted to you while describing your wow factor. Enter 0 if they explicitly told you it was a bad idea or had a negative reaction. Enter 10 if their reaction was something along the lines of "Wow! That's a great idea. I will be a customer. When are you launching it?"

Once everyone in the group has been given a score, compute the average score and enter that value in step 8, in the Virality Score Spreadsheet figure.

STEP 6: AFFORDABILITY SCORE

It is common for affordability to be the reason why even the most passionate day 1 customers may not experience your wow factor.

You need to come up with the best estimate of what you will be charging customers for your wow factor when it is launched. Instead of meticulously calculating the exact dollar amount, you can work with a ballpark figure. Is it going to be in the range of $1, $10, $100, or thousands of dollars?

For every person in step 5 who showed a high level of passion for your wow factor, ask them, "Would you be able to pay X dollars for the product?"

Scoring: Enter a score between 0 and 1. Score 0 if the customers you speak to react negatively to the price point. Enter a maximum score of 1 if they sound like they would comfortably be willing to pay that price range for your wow factor.

Continuing with the pizza story mentioned earlier, let's consider that the restaurant priced their pizza at $1,000 a slice because they used a very expensive secret ingredient imported from Antarctica to make their magical pizza. In this scenario, Jane would not be a day 1 customer. Regardless of how amazing their pizza was, it is very unlikely that a college student working as a tourist guide in New York City would be able to afford $1,000 for a meal.

A $1,000 pizza would probably be a candidate for a completely different day 1 customer group. At this price point, you might have to find your day 1 customers in the billionaire row of New York City.

STEP 7: REACHABILITY SCORE

For each person listed in step 5, enter a score of 0–1, indicating how easy it will be for you to reach this day 1 customer.

In order to do business with your day 1 customers, you have to be able to reach them. In the hypothetical example from step 6, if you believe the right day 1 customer for your $1,000 pizza slice is going to come from the billionaire row in New York, do you know anyone from there? Billionaires are not only busy but also well-guarded. It is not going to be easy to reach them. Do you have any friends or contacts who can get you an in-person meeting to interview them early enough at the ideation phase? If not, it probably will be a tough nut to crack.

On the other hand, if your target day 1 customers are college students, you will face no difficulty in reaching them. However, the affordability of the product plays a crucial role in determining who your ideal day 1 customer will be and how easy it will be to reach this group.

STEP 8: VIRALITY SCORE

The end of your quest to find your wow factor and the right day 1 customer is here. This is the final step to assess whether you have the right day 1 customer group and how likely they are going to help you achieve virality.

Based on the scores from the previous steps, use the next equation to calculate the virality score for each of the three day 1 customer groups.

Virality score = (Passion for wow factor average score) × (Network strength score) × (Reachability average score) × (Affordability average score)

As shown in the figure below, enter each group's score for all the listed criteria that we covered in the previous steps. All of the key criteria are listed in their respective columns in the spreadsheet shown next.

Day 1 Customer Virality Assessment

Group #	Group Name	Virality Score (0–20)	Networking Strength Score (0–2)	Passion for Wow Average Score (0–10)	Affordability Average Score (0–1)	Reachability Average Score (0–1)
1						
2						
3						

Virality Score Spreadsheet

Scoring: Based on the aforementioned equation, a viral score is calculated for each group name mentioned in the spreadsheet. This score will be in the range of 0–20.

Here are the three Virality Score Rules for the right day 1 customer:

1. Any group having a passion score below 7 is considered a bad day 1 customer.

2. In the event that all your day 1 customer groups end up with a low passion score (below 7), it is a strong indication that your market does not consider your feature idea to be a wow factor. Continue exploring other wow factor ideas!

3. Practically speaking, the right day 1 customer group to go to market with your wow factor is the one with the highest virality score. The minimum virality score of 7 is needed to be considered as a viable day 1 customer and wow factor!

Who's Your Day 1 Customer?

Starting a business with the goal to serve everyone from the very first day is not the best approach because "when you try to appeal to everyone, you appeal to no one." Therefore, it is paramount to find the right day 1 customer who will not just appreciate your wow factor but also spread the word about it to everyone they know.

The journey of finding the right day 1 customer starts with learning about the Total Addressable Market. It tells you whether or not it's financially viable to take your wow factor to the market and build your business. Once you have got a high TAM score, it's time to select the day 1 customer groups. Some of these groups might have people who are well-connected and very social. They are more likely to make your wow factor go viral. Another important thing to check for is how passionate the day 1 customer group is about your wow element. But remember that passion alone cannot influence the purchase decision because affordability of the wow factor also plays a crucial role.

It is imperative to diligently follow all the steps outlined in this chapter if your goal is to discover the ideal day 1 customer who will accelerate the growth of your business to virality.

Now that we have all the key ingredients put together, let's take a look at how to build the most valuable product that your market will crave for.

CHAPTER 10 – KEY TAKEAWAYS

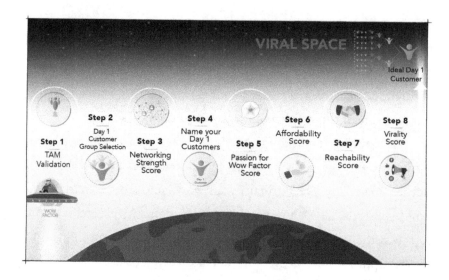

YOUR NOTES

_____

_____

_____

_____

_____

_____

_____

_____

_____

_____

_____

PART III

THE SUCCEED-FASTER EXECUTION

*Learn the in-depth **executional** framework & tools required to succeed faster and win consistently*

Pick the Right Battle at the Right Time

*because every great idea comes
with its expiration date.*

*Stay focused on the most important priority
that will leap you toward your destination
on a daily basis to succeed faster.*

CHAPTER 11

MOST VALUABLE PRODUCT (MVP)

The rapid journey to success begins with a clear definition of what success means for you. As Tony Robbins says, "50% of the process of succeeding is to clearly define what success means." Tony Robbins is one of the most famous motivational speakers and authors in the world.

If you have made it this far in the book, then you must have all the key components that make up a well-articulated definition of success for you. Now, it is important to bring it all together in a concise, powerful, and shareable format so that everybody on your team, including you, is clear on where you are going and what you are building.

But wait, not so fast! There is a very important methodology for managing product development that badly needs an upgrade.

Redefining the MVP

Conventional product development strategies have long favored the concept of Minimum Viable Product (MVP). This methodology advocates for building a product with the bare essentials needed to satisfy the early adopters and then iterating based on customer feedback to make improvements.

While this approach can reduce the time-to-market and initial development costs for a product, it leaves considerable gaps in customer satisfaction and value proposition. In an increasingly competitive and consumer-centric market landscape, this method just won't cut it.

I strongly believe that a minimum viable product will not excite anyone, and it will certainly not help you get the right feedback to develop further. If you are building something new and want your customers to be "wowed," then your product should address the pain points in a manner that has never been done before. Therefore, I submit to you that:

MVP must be redefined to mean "Most Valuable Product" if your goal is to succeed faster at innovation. This upgraded version of MVP should be the new gold standard for developing any product or business.

If you want to achieve your big goals faster, then you have to replace the concept of "minimum viable" with "most valuable." The idea behind this new MVP is to build the most valuable parts or features of your product in each phase of the development cycle so that you have the best chance to wow your customers. After all, who wants a minimum viable anything today?

Remember that your first impression might as well be the last one, and a negative first impression can severely damage your reputation.

Launching another "me too" product to the market will ensure that your offering goes unnoticed. Without proper attention and building momentum rapidly, your business stands no chance of delivering the success that it needs in its limited runway.

Replacing the traditional MVP with the new definition of MVP isn't just a semantic wordplay. It is a strategic overhaul that empowers you with the right mindset and strategy needed to create products that will align with consumer needs and establish a brand synonymous with quality and value.

The Makeup of Your MVP

Now, it's time to bring together the top-down definition of success that you have learnt and hopefully practiced through your journey in this book. We will pack it all together in a summarized and shareable format that will act as a blueprint to help you and your team members build a successful product or business.

ZEITGEIST

At the highest level in the makeup of your MVP lies the concept of zeitgeist, which we have introduced in chapter 1. At any given time, several zeitgeists or megatrends could co-exist across different domains and regions worldwide. You must clearly state the zeitgeist that you want to tap into.

VISION STATEMENT

The next element in the makeup of your MVP is the vision statement. You need to create a strong vision statement for your product or business idea. As discussed in chapter 8, a strong vision is ambitious but achievable, specific, long-term, and well aligned with the chosen zeitgeist.

DAY 1 CUSTOMER PROFILE

The Day 1 Customer Profile is a comprehensive snapshot of the ideal customer for your product or business. Choosing the right day 1 customer can make you go viral. To learn more on how to find the right day 1 customer, you can refer to chapter 10 in this book.

MARKET OPPORTUNITY

The total addressable market size plays a key role in assessing the feasibility of your product or business idea. You also need to specify your one-year and three-year revenue goals after factoring in the TAM score to define success from a financial standpoint.

WOW FACTORS

Wow factors are features that can evoke a "wow" response from your customers once they experience your offering. You must list up to three important wow factors for your product with their descriptions, target date, and success owner. You can refer to chapter 9 to learn how to find your wow factor.

DEAL BREAKERS

Deal breakers are features that you cannot launch your product or business without. You need to specify the top three deal breakers for your product with their descriptions, target date, and success owner. To learn more about deal breakers, refer to chapter 8 in this book.

FEAR FACTORS

You need to list down your fearful thoughts in the form of "what if" questions that are stopping you from building your product or business. To evaluate the accuracy of your fears, you have to give a score for their likelihood of occurrence and severity of impact and then come up with "How Do I" solutions. You can refer to chapter 5 to learn more on how to process your fears.

Now that you are familiar with the makeup of your MVP, you can refer to the MVP summary provided on the next page to solidify your definition of success. This one-page blueprint will act as a guiding light for anyone who becomes a part of your mission. It will clearly describe the "What," "Why," and "Who" of your mission. You and your team members can place the MVP summary sheet in front of your desks as a daily reminder so that everybody on your team is moving in the same direction toward the end goal.

Most Valuable Product (MVP) Summary

Build the most valuable parts or features of your product in each phase

Date :

Time :

A. Zeitgeist

B. Vision Statement

C. Day 1 Customer Profile

D. Market Opportunity

Total Addressable Market:

1 Year Revenue Goal:

3 Year Revenue Goal:

E. Wow Factors

Title	Description	Target Date	Success Owner
1			
2			
3			

F. Deal Breakers

Title	Description	Target Date	Success Owner
1			
2			
3			

G. Fear Factors

What if Concerns	Likelihood of Occurrence (0-100)	Severity of Impact (0-10)	How do I Solutions
1			
2			
3			

[MVP does right]

303

Time to Execute Your Dream Now

Defining the MVP is paramount not just for you but also for your stakeholders and the team members you'll be onboarding to bring your dream to life. You will be operating most efficiently only when all stakeholders and team members are putting their collective energies into moving ahead in the same direction toward the final destination. When people channel their efforts in different directions without proper guidance, it leads to a waste of time and resources. The lack of clarity and focus is the main reason why most businesses end up losing out during the execution phase, even though they have the best vision and wow factors.

By summarizing the definition of success with our Most Valuable Product Summary, you have already made 50 percent of the progress. The remaining 50 percent requires you to assemble a team and start executing on your idea. Hiring the right people to build your dream requires a significant upfront investment, and many of you might lack adequate financial support. The good news is that there are investors who can fund your dream if you show them the true potential of your business idea.

To be honest, convincing investors to fund your dream is a tough nut to crack because there are many other founders looking to secure funding for their businesses. After helping dozens of entrepreneurs successfully build their innovation prototypes and raising funds from investors, I have a few useful tips that can help you secure a budget to give your idea a runway to have a chance at success.

CHAPTER 11 – KEY TAKEAWAYS

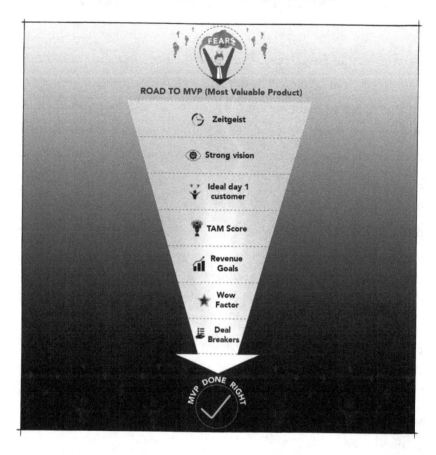

YOUR NOTES

_____

_____

_____

_____

_____

_____

_____

_____

_____

CHAPTER 12

HOW TO FUND YOUR DREAM

The journey to building your Most Valuable Product requires plenty of resources, and you will need sufficient fuel in the form of money to stay in motion till you reach your destination.

As the research conducted by Bill Gross of Idealab suggests, money does not guarantee success, not even close.[7] However, not having the right level of funding at the right time is certainly a deal breaker for everybody. Without money, you cannot pay for the resources, team members, and everything else needed to stay in business.

While having money doesn't guarantee success, not having it ensures that you won't remain in business to have a chance at succeeding.

---

7   Bill Gross, "The single biggest reason why start-ups succeed," YouTube, July 1, 2015, https://www.youtube.com/watch?v=bNpx7gpSqbY.

Funding Can Be a Deal Breaker

A majority of startups are bootstrapped in the early stages of their journey, but as they grow, the capital requirements far exceed what they have at their disposal. At this point, finding investors who might be interested in your idea and can provide adequate capital to keep you in the game becomes a necessity.

What's very interesting about fundraising and investors is that when your business actually needs the money, they are unwilling to bear the risk and invest in it, but when it's doing great and you don't need external capital, everybody wants to invest in your venture. In my experience, it's always good to have money before you need it because when you are desperately looking for it, you won't get it fast enough to keep your business afloat.

Raising funds from investors can feel like begging—especially if you don't come from the world of finance and are not used to asking for money. In this chapter, I will share the ten rules that I have summarized to help you maximize your chances of winning over investors so that you can stay in business long enough to improve your likelihood of succeeding.

Money Is Like Energy

Before we dig deeper into how you can successfully raise funds for your business or project, it is critical to understand how money works. **Very much like the laws of physics, money is like energy: It can neither be created nor be destroyed.** It can only change hands or be transferred from one bank account to another.

I know we can argue that governments or central banks can regulate monetary supply, but let's keep governing bodies out for the simplicity of this conversation. Regular civilians, entrepreneurs, and corporate leaders do not have the ability to create or destroy money. We can only provide something of value that makes people willing to exchange their money for it.

As a consumer, you should always seek value over price because the price is not as much about what you actually pay as it is about the value you get in return. Most investors are smart consumers who are concerned about the value they stand to gain from investing in your business rather than the amount of money you're seeking.

To secure funds for your business, you must understand how investors think and the criteria they follow to write the investment check. Your goal should be to create a startup that can deliver something valuable. More importantly, you must develop a well-articulated perception of that value and effectively communicate it to your audience.

Many startup founders struggle to raise capital because they fail to effectively convey how their unique value proposition will benefit consumers. Ultimately, investors back your business because they believe it will generate a good return on their investment. If you fail to convince them, they will look for other promising opportunities.

Begging for Money?

I have an engineering background, so building things comes naturally to me, but asking for money does not. If you are like me or most other startup founders, you probably don't view seeking funds from investors in a positive light. Initially, I used to believe that if you build something great, investors will chase you to fund your business idea. Over the years, I found that the reality is quite different, and 99 percent of startups have to "beg" for money. Yes, I said beg. If you don't come from the world of finance, raising money can literally feel like begging.

For my first company, I bootstrapped the funding using what my wife and I had saved from years of working in corporate jobs. Fortunately, the business model I put in place was generating cash so quickly that we never had to rely on external investments. However, for another venture where we were developing a deep-tech product, I needed to raise outside capital because I ran out of funds after spending a substantial amount on the prototype. My desire to see this big dream succeed far outweighed the negative perception of raising funds from investors. I rolled up my sleeves and embarked on an eye-opening journey of fundraising.

There is no question that raising capital is more difficult than most people think it is. Initially, I received a lot of "Nos," so much that I got to the point where I stopped counting. I learned a lot about the dos and don'ts of fundraising from an entrepreneur's perspective throughout this journey. I had to digest everything I learned and make it happen for my new visionary startup. Eventually, I applied the valuable lessons learnt from all the painful rejections to get my first breakthrough.

In the past eight years, I have learned some important fundraising principles after helping over dozens of tech startups and entrepreneurs in their pursuit of raising capital. I have worked as an advisor and as a paid consultant to help startups, including one of my own, successfully pitch their idea and raise capital from investors.

If I had known and followed the principles of winning investors in the beginning of my journey, I would have been super successful at raising capital when it was most needed. However, in the end, I am grateful I didn't raise the money too soon because I would have wasted it on the wrong priorities. If you want to secure funds for your business, you must learn about the different stages of fundraising and how they work.

Three Stages of Fundraising

The requirements for capital can vary depending on where you are in your entrepreneurial journey. Understanding the different fundraising stages will give you more clarity on how to raise funds successfully. In this section, we will explore three different stages of fundraising. You must note that there can be more stages from a technical stand-point, but for the sake of simplicity, we will only focus on the three important ones.

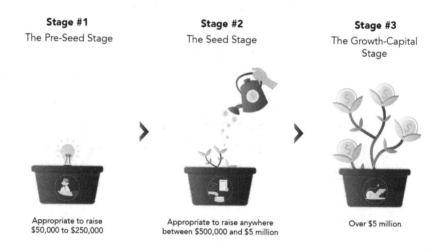

Stage #1
The Pre-Seed Stage

Stage #2
The Seed Stage

Stage #3
The Growth-Capital Stage

Appropriate to raise $50,000 to $250,000

Appropriate to raise anywhere between $500,000 and $5 million

Over $5 million

STAGE #1: THE PRE-SEED STAGE

This stage is the one where you have an idea on paper, a high-level understanding of your market, and a rough hypothesis about your business model. At this level, you need to have enough money to build a basic prototype, conduct customer research, and learn about the product market fit. Generally, this stage is bootstrapped by the founder or funded by "friends and family." If you are like me or most other startup founders, you probably don't have rich or particularly generous friends and family members. Besides bootstrapping, you can rely on startup accelerators and angel investors who specialize in this stage. It would be appropriate to raise anywhere between $50,000 and $250,000 and perhaps do a few more rounds to keep the momentum going.

STAGE #2: THE SEED STAGE

At this point, investors expect you to have a working prototype of the idea and some valuable proof of concept. You should have begun product market fit and have a few paid pilots and Letters of Intent (LOIs) to validate the market demand for your product. As a bonus, you may also have booked some revenue for your product, but the annual recurring revenue figure should be less than $1 million. If you are solving a deep-tech problem, you should ideally have created some valuable intellectual property or filed for a relevant patent(s). It would be appropriate to raise anywhere between $500,000 and $5 million at this stage. If you are a deep-tech or deep-science product company, then you are going to be on the higher end of the seed capital range. Other companies, especially software and online-based, will be in the $500,000 to $2 million range.

STAGE #3: THE GROWTH CAPITAL STAGE

You only qualify for growth capital after you have established product market fit and shown persistent sales/revenue growth of your products. Generally speaking, you need to be over $1 million in annual recurring revenue from several customers to show a confident and sustainable growth pattern. This established growth curve demonstrates that there is an unquestionable demand for your product, and customers are not hesitant to pay for it.

Passionate testimonials can also be very helpful as they act like strong social proof. At this point, you should have enough sales track record to plot revenue and trace customer acquisition growth that has already happened. You can extrapolate from that to confidently show growth projections for the next three to five years. The primary reason to raise funds at this stage is to fuel the resources needed in your trajectory to achieve or outperform your projections. This capital will primarily be deployed to significantly grow the company's top line; hence the name "Growth Capital."

It can start at $5 million and go up all the way to the big billions. There are several classes of growth capital: Series A, B, C, and so on. I will not get into the intricacies of growth capital in this chapter. If you want to learn more about funding your startup, I highly recommend a book called *Venture Deals* by Brad Feld and Jason Mendelson. You will learn everything you need to know about fundraising for startups. It is a very technical book, so I had to read it several times to really understand and internalize all the concepts. I recommend this book because I believe it's the best crash course on fundraising that I have come across.

The Ten Rules to Winning Over Investors for Seed Capital

Embarking on the journey of securing seed capital is a pivotal chapter in every entrepreneur's story. It can totally change the course of your business and influence your growth trajectory. Therefore, it is important to learn some critical rules that will help you win over investors and secure your seed capital easily.

SEED INVESTOR RULE #1: SALES TRUMPS EVERYTHING ELSE WITH INVESTORS

This rule applies ubiquitously to all startups who are seeking funds from investors, regardless of their target market and area of expertise. Ultimately, all investors want to grow their money multiple folds. It is very hard to convince any investor to fund your startup without having any proof of sales. The more sales your business generates, the easier it will be for you to get the required capital and expand further. The opportunity cost for any investor to miss out on a sales-generating startup is too high. So, if investors don't believe in your idea, don't work too hard to convince them. Go sell and let the numbers do the talking.

SEED INVESTOR RULE #2: PRODUCT MARKET FIT AND DETAILED CUSTOMER INSIGHTS ARE THE NEXT BEST THING

If you are at a stage where you haven't generated any sales yet, then your detailed target market insights and product market fit become your best proof to convince investors. You need to show where you fit in this market and also provide the customers' insights gathered from conversations on a ground level. You should also be able to produce proof that your market is interested in your idea. This could be in the form of small paid or unpaid pilots (paid is preferable), LOIs, and anything that is more than just anecdotal. It is important to remember that investors aren't solely funding your business because they believe in your product. They invest because they are convinced that the target market is captivated by your exciting idea, and it holds the potential to generate revenue and gain financial momentum with their capital backing.

SEED INVESTOR RULE #3: BUSINESS DEVELOPMENT FOUNDERS OR EMPLOYEES ARE REQUIRED BEFORE RAISING YOUR SEED MONEY

As I learned from one of my favorite mentors and colleagues, there is a big difference between a salesperson and a business development professional. While the former is focused on closing individual deals and transactions, the latter takes a broader approach to fostering strategic partnerships that drive sustained growth. Investors are not just looking for a product with high potential; they are seeking a well-rounded team that can navigate the complexities of business expansion.

In the dynamic landscape of startup fundraising, having experienced business development personnel in your team before seeking seed money can increase the likelihood of success. These individuals know how to identify, negotiate, and forge alliances that extend beyond immediate sales. They possess the strategic vision to spot opportunities for collaboration, co-marketing, and distribution, all of which can exponentially amplify your market reach and revenue potential.

SEED INVESTOR RULE #4: HAVE A CLEAR AND CONCISE PLAN

You should always draft a clear, concise, and convincing plan, even if it's not your best. It should address important questions like how you are going to make money, what you will build, why your market needs your product, and most importantly, how you will deploy the funds to execute the plan. Even if your plan isn't in its final form, investors are more inclined to back individuals who present a well-thought-out plan with a clear strategy for execution rather than those without any plan at all.

SEED INVESTOR RULE #5: INVESTORS ARE LIKE WOLVES—THEY MOVE IN PACKS

Investors are like wolves: they move in packs and invest in groups. The hardest part about raising money is finding a leader in the pack who is interested in your business idea and ready to invest first. Once you have convinced the lead investor, it's easy to get others in that "pack" to follow in their footsteps. When I started my fundraising journey, I was stunned to see how easy it was to meet investors and pitch them your idea. They are happy to spare thirty minutes of their time to learn about your startup. But most of them will say something like, "We don't lead rounds" or "We don't invest in hardware." They will ask you to find a lead investor first, and then they will be happy to invest.

SEED INVESTOR RULE #6: FIND YOUR LEAD INVESTOR

The investor community is very close-knit and highly focused. Some of them are quite specific about which industry they will choose and at what stage of the company they will invest in. Many established ones take it a step further and will tell you: "We don't lead rounds" (as I mentioned in rule #5). I had no clue what it meant when I heard it for the very first time. But after doing some research, I learned that most investors are unwilling to take the risk of going first. They prefer to avert the hard job of establishing the right valuation for the company. Therefore, many large investors, including institutional ones, say, "Find a reputable investor to lead, and we will follow." I know it's weird, but that's how this industry works. Most investors are risk-averse, and only a few visionary leaders have the courage and smarts to support visionary dreamers.

Generally speaking, you may need to find niche Venture Capital (VC) firms specializing in your industry and seed-stage companies. Alternatively, you can rely on high-net-worth investors who believe in your idea and are willing to take a risk.

SEED INVESTOR RULE #7: RECRUIT AN INVESTMENT BANKER AS A KEY ADVISOR

Learning how to communicate with prospective investors and pitch your idea can be a challenging journey. If you need to get funds and don't have the time to learn the process, it's always a good idea to hire an investment banker who has a solid network and specializes in dealing with your target lead investors. However, be extremely careful here. Unfortunately, I have come across many investment bankers in New York City (where I'm based) who were flat-out crooks. They are happy to charge you a high monthly retainer, tell you a bunch of lies, and ask for commission and equity for doing absolutely nothing but BS.

Hiring the right investment banker as your key advisor is important as they will help you connect with investors who are more inclined to invest in your business. You can hire them as a paid or an unpaid advisor (depending on their expectation), and they will guide you through the process. Anyone looking for high retainers at this stage is a huge red flag. A seasoned and confident investment banker will generally ask for a small monthly retainer to cover the basic expenses of their time, but they can ask you for a success fee on the rise, which is typically 5 percent and can go up to 8 percent. They might also look up to some equity, typically between 0.5 and 2 percent, earned on your success or over time.

You must ensure that the person you are planning to hire as an advisor has a proven track record of raising seed capital either as an investment banker or as a serial entrepreneur. You do not want a rookie pretending to be an expert who is learning at your expense. If you end up hiring the wrong person, cut them loose as soon as you realize that they may not be legit. The time you spend dealing with the wrong advisor could have been spent with the right one, who might have helped you achieve your fundraising goals.

SEED INVESTOR RULE #8: HAVE A FOUNDER-DRIVEN PITCH

Regardless of how amazing your team members and advisors are, investors will expect the founder(s) to deliver the pitch—a solid and convincing one. If you are the only founder and your pitching skills aren't great, start practicing or find a co-founder who is good at it. Investors will likely not invest in a seed-stage company, even if you're making millions of dollars and taking off like a rocket ship unless at least one of the founders is charismatic and can represent the company and its ideas eloquently. This is where the right investment banker can save the day. They can go on a pitching spree with investors who are not likely to invest in you or whom you wouldn't worry about burning. Yes, it is extremely easy to get a meeting with an investor. They almost never turn down requests from startups. Identify the investors you don't mind burning, or sign up for pitch competitions to learn and practice more.

SEED INVESTOR RULE #9: FUNDRAISE FOR EIGHTEEN MONTHS OF RUNWAY

In the seed stage, you should plan to focus on raising ample funds to secure an eighteen-month runway for your startup. In other words, you must be able to identify your monthly burn, create an execution plan for building the product, and should aim to generate at least $1 million in annual recurring revenue. You have to show how the amount you are asking for will cover all expenses for at least eighteen months to achieve a point of financial sustainability where your business is generating sufficient cash flow to keep growing. Alternatively, you can achieve significant progress within the first twelve to fourteen months following your seed fundraising to make yourself eligible for the growth capital round.

But why eighteen months? Well, because it gives you twelve to fourteen months to achieve the revenue goals needed to qualify for a growth capital round. You can use the next four to six months to raise funds in this round. Doing this will ensure that your company doesn't die young while it's growing rapidly just because you didn't time the fundraising correctly.

SEED INVESTOR RULE #10: BUILD A FOCUSED AND STANDARD INVESTOR PITCH DECK

The significance of a well-crafted investor pitch deck cannot be overstated when it comes to securing the seed capital for your startup. A focused pitch deck communicates your business's value proposition, market opportunity, competitive advantage, market strategy, and financial projections with clarity and precision. It serves as a gateway, inviting potential investors to delve deeper into your venture. Based on my experience, investors look for the following topics to be covered in a pitch deck:

- Problem

- Solution (clear articulation of your unique value proposition and your day 1 customer)

- Showcase Product Videos/Mockups and Demos

- The Grand Long-term Vision

- TAM and SOM (include a worksheet in the appendix to explain and show the metrics and how you arrived at these numbers)

- Competitors and Your Competitive Advantage

- Customer Insights Stats and Customer Quotes

- Go-to-Market Strategy and Sales Funnel

- Unit Economics

- Team

- Use of Funds

It is important to distill your business idea into a concise, compelling, and visually engaging presentation. Remember that your pitch deck is your business's first handshake with investors, so make it count!

FUNDING YOUR WAY TO SUCCESS

Many startup founders venture out to solve an existing problem in a way that has never been done before. They set ambitious goals that are hard to accomplish, but it can be highly rewarding if done right. Over 90 percent of startups fail to achieve their mission and have to say goodbye to their ambitious goals. It is important to note that achieving a major goal requires a great team, and without adequate financing, you can't afford to hire the right people.

As we have learned in this chapter, it is critical for both startup founders and intrapreneurs in big companies to learn how to win investors and convince their board. Only then can they get the necessary funding to build a resilient team and deliver on their grandiose dream.

Now, it's time to turn the page to the final chapter and learn how to build your dream team that will execute your wow factor and make the tough journey with you to see your vision come to life.

CHAPTER 12 – KEY TAKEAWAYS

TEN RULES TO WINNING OVER INVESTORS

1. Sales trumps everything for investors
2. Customer insights is the next best option for investors
3. Need a business development person before the seed round
4. Clear and concise business plan
5. Investors are like wolves: They move in packs
6. Find your lead investor
7. Find a reliable and trustable investment banker
8. Founder led pitch
9. Fundraise for eighteen months of runway
10. Build a focused investor pitch deck

YOUR NOTES

_____
_____
_____
_____
_____
_____
_____
_____
_____
_____
_____
_____

Succeed Faster **SECRET #10**

Build a Burn-On Team

*instead of the typical burnt-out team by
going fast and far with the right people
to succeed faster with your vision.*

CHAPTER 13

BUILD A BURN-ON TEAM

The path to virality for a new product or business is not a straight and easy line. It consists of waves of ups and downs that have the potential to shake out the majority. Each wave will wash out most people, leaving only the few who are able and willing to take on the next wave of expansion. As the famous African proverb goes: "If you want to go fast, go alone. If you want to go far, go together."

In short, you cannot build anything meaningful all by yourself. You will need a team that sticks together and goes through the journey with you. However, it is very challenging to build such teams today as people's attention span is getting shorter by the year, and the culture of instant gratification has become the new normal. The majority of teams get burnt out and move on to their next gig within just a year or two if not months. In fact, there is an entirely new type of economy that has emerged, and it is called the gig economy. While this may be a great solution for simple services in a time when labor shortages are rampant because of aging demographics, it is not conducive to long-term innovation and meaningful evolution.

I have been leading teams since the age of twenty-one. In the past two decades, I have directly and indirectly led over a thousand people on big missions at all levels of organizations. Over the years, I have experienced both failures and successes with different team settings, as diverse as Texas and Indonesia. It is from this point of view that I submit to you, the African proverb needs an evolution to a more modern and effective version:

"To go fast, go alone. To go far, go together. **But to go fast and far, go together *with the right people*.**"

Building anything innovative with sustainable long-term success does not only require you to go far, but it also demands you to go fast enough to compete and stay in business before your runway expires. This path is long and complex, so you cannot make it by yourself. While you cannot build your grand vision alone, you also will never achieve any meaningful success with the wrong team members, as they will get burnt out of the game fast. When things get tough, which they will, a burnt-out team loses focus and the positive energy needed to make the necessary breakthroughs. Typically, emotions run hot, and the culture can turn toxic and highly unproductive if the team members can't quit because of monetary or contractual reasons.

On the contrary, with a burn-on team, the worst-case scenario is that you will have brought together the most valuable team members with whom you will enjoy traversing the tough journey toward your vision. Lifelong bonds are likely to form and you take on many other missions in the future with your most valuable team. In the best-case scenario, you will earn everything from the worst case plus a much higher probability of burning on through the multiple waves of expansion to get to your end goal rapidly, assuming you got the zeitgeist, wow factor, and the ideal day 1 customer right. I am not saying this just based on my personal experience. The data backs it up.

In Bill Gross's study of two hundred startups, "Team" was ranked as the second-most important factor that determines a company's success.

Five Key Determinants of Startup Success

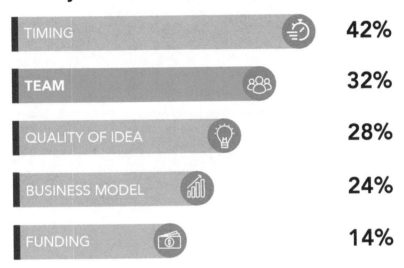

TIMING	42%
TEAM	32%
QUALITY OF IDEA	28%
BUSINESS MODEL	24%
FUNDING	14%

Bill Gross's Study of Two Hundred Startups

There are various reasons why highly skilled teams can become dysfunctional: people in mismatched roles, foundational skill gaps, poor work ethics, overly competitive individuals, clash of egos, political culture, weak leadership, low motivation, disparate vision/values, and the list can go on and on. In a world where people lack the patience and funding for unproven innovation, the few who get their fair shot fail often because even if they manage to not run out of time and money, their teams burn out sooner rather than later.

Virtually everybody will tell you that you need to put together a great team to build a great business. But what they don't tell you is how to exactly do it. Assembling such an impactful group of people who can burn on through the difficult journey toward success is very tricky. The detailed blueprint for building and running such a great burn-on team would require an entire book by itself. Therefore, in this final chapter, I will leave you with the ten most important rules to get you on the right track to build your own burn-on team.

The Ten Rules to Build and Keep a Burn-On Team

BURN-ON TEAM RULE #1: Build your Most Valuable Team (MVT) first.

The composition of your team can be the wow factor or the deal breaker for your mission. Build the most valuable team (MVT), and you will significantly improve your odds of succeeding. The MVT is the most compact yet the most extraordinary group of people who complement one another to burn on through all the obstacles to get to your destination faster.

As a highly valuable and functional team, they possess all the necessary skills to build out the company vision rapidly. The first step toward creating the MVT is to clearly define the skills needed in all the different highly focused areas of capabilities. Ideally, you should have each team member dedicated to one core area and nothing else because focus accelerates progress! However, if you have a tight budget, you can group some complementary skills and find the right candidate to take up this combined responsibility as long as they possess the necessary core skills in all the functional areas they oversee.

The number of people needed to form an MVT can vary depending on your goal and timeline. Generally speaking, startups should aim for a maximum of five members, while businesses that have passed their initial phases might stretch to ten members in the MVT. A team of three is considered ideal for building an MVT in the early stages. It is important to note that a business leader should not have more than ten direct reportees. Most important, your MVT members may not be well-known and highly experienced or have advanced skills yet, but they *must* be amazing at the basics and be fully committed to achieving the product or business's vision.

329

As an unbreakable rule, avoid filling a position that reports to you directly unless you or a trusted MVT leader has the time to provide guidance and hold that person accountable.

Before allowing your MVT members to hire for their respective teams, make sure they have demonstrated the highest level of productivity in their functional area and consistently shown commitment to your mission through a few challenging times.

Avoid making the mistake of giving new hires at lower levels of the organization a bad or unproven boss. It is the best way to destroy your brand culture and market reputation when scaling.

The next nine rules will provide you with the specific guidelines to build your MVT that will burn on through the waves of ups and downs to achieve your end goal.

BURN-ON TEAM RULE #2: Articulate your purpose, and ensure it matches with the purpose of your MVT members.

A team built on shared values is more likely to work together in the long run. When you have a well-defined purpose, you can screen potential candidates to identify those whose personal values have enough of an overlap with the core values of your company. Refer to the Most Valuable Product (MVP) 1 Page Summary in chapter 11. It will help you clearly articulate a consistent message on why your business exists, where it is heading, and what exactly it is going to do. When team members genuinely connect with the broader vision and purpose of your company, their work takes on a deeper meaning. Also, people who strongly believe in your cause and are highly passionate about achieving those goals are less likely to burn out, even during the most difficult times.

It's very unlikely to find team members who will have the exact same purpose as you because they can be in a different phase of their lives and might have varied aspirations. But as long as there is sufficient alignment on your business's destination and theirs, you can hire them. What you want them to do for your mission should help them achieve their personal aspirations as well. If not, they will never be as committed to your company's vision as you need them to be.

Let's say you are planning to hire an amazing software engineer with the core skills needed for the role and a great personality as part of your core team. However, their purpose in life right now is to settle down, build a family, and have a great work-life balance. On the other hand, you are on a mission to build the most admired brand in the world that grows from millions to billions of dollars very rapidly. While this person may be more than capable for the job, you will likely need someone who can be fully focused and go above and beyond to manage very tight deadlines. This engineer, even though on paper is amazing for the job, is likely going to get burnt out and will not be able to keep up with the pace of the rest of the team because your purpose and theirs isn't aligned at this point in time. Therefore, it will likely create a lot of resentment and mismatched expectations, and inadvertently bring negative energy to the team that can impact the culture of the entire organization.

It is important to note that people's purpose and goals can change over time. They might not prioritize the same things in the next three to five years, so it's crucial to not solely focus on what they have accomplished in the past.

The past should surely be a consideration, but focus more on understanding their vision and commitment for the next three to five years.

BURN-ON TEAM RULE #3: Be diligent in ensuring all hires possess strong foundational skills for the job.

The first step to building your burn-on team requires you to clearly define the key job roles and their associated capabilities needed to form your most valuable core team. The core positions are like the vital pillars supporting the structure of your team. You need to pick people who possess the right foundational skill set for these job roles. Only after clearly defining the key skills for the role can you start recruiting the best-fit candidates.

Be very diligent in testing to ensure the candidates have the necessary skills at the level needed to do the job. This is a non-negotiable, and when in doubt, DO NOT hire.

Many make the mistake of hiring individuals just based on their work experience and résumés. I'm not undermining the importance of experience. But if a candidate's résumé doesn't translate into them having the core foundational skills needed for the job, it is guaranteed to be a struggle. Teaching someone core skills for a job can be a long-term coaching project that you do not have time for. Also, you may not possess that skill on your team currently to be able to teach it to anyone new. Therefore, you should never compromise on core skills because nothing meaningful will get done fast enough, even if they are the most experienced and the hardest-working people on the planet.

In the event that you are not 100 percent convinced whether the candidate is strong at the core capabilities for the job, always do a paid trial for one day with the candidate.

Pay the candidate as a freelancer to work for you for a full day. On that day, give them a real-life assignment for their role, and collaborate with them. Make sure to create challenging and respectfully confrontational situations to see how they react.

At the end of the one-day trial, it will be very clear whether the candidate is the right fit for the job or not. If you are still not 100 percent sure, pass on the candidate before confirmation bias takes over to satisfy your desperation to fill the role.

The seeker mindset (chapter 2) should be a core skill required for every team member of any innovative project or business. No matter how strong they are with the known core skills, there will always be new challenges because such is the nature of innovation. It will require the team members to learn new skills rapidly. If the candidate is not proficient at troubleshooting and on-the-job learning, then their experience won't be of much value.

Hire a strong candidate even if they lack some advanced skills because those can be learned on the job when required. However, you cannot compromise on core foundational skills and the seeker mindset for your MVT.

BURN-ON TEAM RULE #4: Do not use money as the main tool to hire your most valuable team members.

A well-known experiment involving a candle, matches, and a box of thumbtacks helps prove the point that monetary incentives can help you build a more successful team when done right.

This experiment was first conducted by psychologist Karl Duncker in 1945. Mr. Duncker provided the participants with a candle, a matchbox, and a box of thumbtacks. These objects were placed on a table next to a wall. He asked a group of people to solve a problem that involved placing a lit candle on the wall in such a way that it would not drip any wax on the table set underneath it.

This popular experiment had two variations, distinguished by the manner in which thumbtacks were presented to the participants. In the first case, the thumbtacks were placed inside the box, which made it hard for people to visualize it as a tool for solving the problem. Very few were able to come up with a solution in this scenario.

In the second case, Mr. Duncker rearranged these items by placing the thumbtacks on the table instead of keeping them in the box. It gave the appearance of the box itself being a tool, and more participants were able to solve the problem in this setup.

The experiment was repeated again in 1962 by a psychology professor named Sam Glucksberg. This time, one group of participants were offered a monetary reward depending on how quickly they solved the problem. As one might expect, the financial incentive motivated some people to solve the problem faster. However, it only pertained to the group that received the thumbtacks outside the box.

This experiment also had a second variation, wherein the tacks were placed inside the box and not directly on the table. This time, the problem was solved faster by people who were not offered any monetary incentive. Some of those in the incentive group did not succeed at all. It was found that introducing money as an incentive to the experiment blocked creativity in most individuals.

As a startup or a product developer, you need a team that can think outside the box without having a well-defined step-by-step operational process. When you offer financial incentives early on, your team members will look at being more productive instead of being more creative, which might put a damper on innovation. Using money as the main tool to hire important team members may attract the wrong people who are only financially motivated and are not passionate about your mission of solving the market problem.

BURN-ON TEAM RULE #5: Hiring nobody is better than hiring the wrong person for the job.

Timing is very important for achieving any goal, especially in a competitive business environment or when funding is limited. Quite often, we end up hiring people without thoroughly and honestly vetting them out because of some perceived sense of urgency driven by the pressure to deliver a win within a deadline. Hiring the wrong individual for a role on your core team is guaranteed to yield poor results in the short term and a bad team culture in the long run. This is obvious in hindsight but not apparent in the pressure of the moment.

Bad hires can be a major distraction, not just for the business function you are hiring them for but also for the person they report to and other members on the core team. A bad hire will require you to spend a lot of time coaching them, but you will also need to do their job as they will not be productive. In the meantime, you still have your job to do. This is not likely to improve over time, even though you may continue to hope that it will until it is too late. It will end up adding more load on you and create lots of negative tension between you and the bad hire. If they are not fired soon enough, this negative tension will permeate across your core team and eventually the entire organization.

Investing in a person who doesn't meet the requirements of the role leads to a waste of time, money, and energy. Remember, life will give you more of what you tolerate. So,

If you are not convinced that a candidate will be a great fit for the role, then keep the position vacant till you find the right person. Set a high bar by not compromising on the standards required to be a member of your MVT.

As a stopgap measure, you can hire a highly qualified advisor or contributor on a freelance basis. Pay them for the part-time role to make progress if required. A qualified advisor is someone who has a lot of experience, has successfully performed in similar positions, and possesses mastery of the skills you are recruiting them for. Perhaps you cannot afford to hire them full-time, or they are not able to provide the commitments you need for the full-time role. Do not hire anyone as an advisor formally until you get to know them well and are able to verify their body of work.

BURN-ON TEAM RULE #6: Hire fast and fire fast is an old and lazy strategy.

Hire fast and fire fast is a very popular mantra in the modern corporate world, especially with people who are obsessed about agility. While we all aspire for agility, hire fast and fire fast is a shortcut solution to a foundational problem. It will end up costing you a lot more in the long term as it is not a sound business strategy. It leads to instability, poor team culture, and damage to the company's reputation.

Rushing to hire out of sheer desperation often leads to a biased perspective, causing you to only see what you need in the short term while potentially overlooking crucial gaps in a candidate's skill set or behavior. This confirmation bias can prove to be a costly mistake. Instead, if you take your time to conduct proper due diligence before hiring your team members, it can save you from firing people and creating a negative sentiment.

To build a burn-on team that sticks together, your goal should always be to hire right before hiring fast. Nothing wrong with hiring fast, but just make sure that it is not at the expense of hiring right.

In case you made any mistakes and hired the wrong person, you have no choice but to fire fast. Holding on to individuals who are clearly unfit for their roles will do more damage than the limited short-term benefits that can come out of it.

Once you realize that you hired the wrong person, go ahead and fire them. However, never view firing positively. Always regret firing, and regard it as a bitter pill needed to fix a mistake. Make sure to reflect and learn from this mistake for the next time.

It is important to accept it and learn from it so that you don't have to frequently fire people after making hiring mistakes. No matter how justified you may be to fire the wrong person fast, other team members do not see firing people in a positive light. It will negatively impact the team spirit and culture when it happens frequently, even if it's not your fault. Strive to improve your hiring process by learning from your past recruitment mistakes. Remember, a team that is nurtured through thoughtful recruitment and development is more likely to endure through challenges and drive to the common vision faster.

In summary, the solution is to

Replace "hire fast and fire fast" with *hire right and regret firing fast*.

BURN-ON TEAM RULE #7: Be ruthlessly agile with mandatory weekly sprints.

Agile is the most popular software development methodology used today to build products and drive innovation across different industries worldwide. In fact, many avant-garde leaders are leveraging agile to build their businesses, and some are even running well-established global companies with agile principles. There are several refreshing concepts in agile that I find very useful and valuable, especially when compared to its predecessor, the traditional waterfall project management method. The main challenge with agile is that it's a loose model that can be adapted in different ways. Quite often, leveraging this framework without a strong vision and a well-articulated wow factor can lead to teams becoming shortsighted and highly operational.

The agile methodology advocates for breaking down a product's definition into smaller iterative features and milestones for its development. Most agile teams operate on a two-week sprint cycle to facilitate product development with this approach. They break down the key features into achievable subparts known as user stories. Throughout the sprint, the team works together on developing, testing, and delivering these user stories that contribute to the larger project objective. As the team successfully completes user stories, their baseline velocity is established. Changes in this metric are tracked over time across sprints. It serves as a quick and accurate measure of the team's momentum, assuming you have correctly implemented rule number 8, mentioned in the next section.

Building the micro features of a product in a frequent iterative cycle seems like an effective approach to developing products. However, having a checkpoint on meaningful accomplishments every two weeks to ensure that you are moving in the right direction is ironically not the most agile way to manage the development of innovative products.

Imagine creating a new product that requires ten iterations to develop, test, and optimize all the features. If your team follows the bimonthly sprints and you assess their performance and deliverables every other week, you are looking at a minimum of twenty weeks to complete the project.

What if you could pack your product development iterations into a more compact time frame? This is possible when you upgrade to a weekly sprint cycle. It would literally cut the time to discover and resolve problems in half. Simultaneously, a weekly sprint cycle will double your productivity and significantly reduce the time to market. It is also easier to manage on the calendar with the same cadence week after week.

Navigating the different stages of ideation, articulation, development, testing, and delivery within just one week consistently may initially appear aggressive, especially if your team has been following the bimonthly sprints for a long time. You will likely face resistance from your team members, who might perceive this model as too fast and unsustainable. However,

Adopting the ruthlessly agile approach of a weekly sprint cadence with your team will cultivate a high-performing team that will burn on through all the obstacles and succeed faster at delivering your vision.

This outcome is guaranteed when you diligently pick the right individuals for your MVT following the criteria in the five rules mentioned previously. Also, if your MVT has the right individuals with solid foundational skills and a seeker's mindset, the initial resistance will quickly turn into excitement and pride when they see a significant productivity boost and a doubling of the speed at which real issues are recognized and resolved.

By transitioning to a weekly sprint model, your team starts and ends a complete development cycle much faster in comparison to the bimonthly sprints. At the beginning of every week, your team should prioritize the most critical tasks and clearly articulate the definition of success for their sprint. The wow factors and deal breakers are diligently broken down into Micro Most Valuable Features (MMVFs) to be delivered weekly.

At the end of the week, every member of your MVT must complete their user stories, demo their accomplishments, and track their velocity compared to the baseline. This practice allows for a focused and rapid evaluation of vital aspects, including your team's velocity, ongoing development efforts, and alignment with the overarching long-term vision on a weekly basis. A journey of a thousand steps requires you to take one step at a time, as efficiently as possible, ensuring each move is in the right direction while progressing toward your destination. This practice will undoubtedly help you establish a more dynamic and responsive team that is required to achieve innovation at a faster pace in the modern era.

BURN-ON TEAM RULE #8: Build a demo culture, and infuse a healthy dose of competition.

Establishing a culture that is centered around showing rather than telling can singularly have the greatest impact on your team's productivity. This can be achieved by having each team member "demo" their stated accomplishment at the end of the weekly sprint cycle and ensuring that it perfectly aligns with your expectations regarding that goal. Quite often, people tend to say that the work is done instead of *showing* how they have contributed or what they have actually achieved. If they are not able to successfully demo their achievements, then the "user stories" cannot be marked as complete or shown in their velocity for the week. There cannot be any compromise here, regardless of why your team members were unable to show what they claimed to have built successfully.

Fostering a demo culture will eliminate all the noise of posturing and reveal the true performance of each team member, giving you the opportunity to correct the course much more frequently. This practice is highly effective because demonstrating individual achievements to the team promotes transparency and instills a deep sense of accountability and competition. It will help you learn what is really missing on a weekly basis so that you can prioritize the most critical aspects of your project for the week ahead. Without this continuous iterative cycle of learning and reprioritization, you will not succeed faster toward achieving your end goal.

If you have multiple teams building different products or working on varied aspects of the same project, organizing a "wow demo" competition can surely infuse excitement. Most important, a healthy dose of cross team competition for the weekly wow demo winner title can work wonders for boosting the productivity of these teams.

At my company Techolution, I run a "wow demo" league every six months where more than a dozen product teams participate to compete for the champion title. In the spirit of this competition, different product teams have to showcase their wow accomplishment of the week to everyone else attending the demo presentation. The attendees present during the session can choose to give a wow response while watching the live demo if they are "wowed" by what they are watching. At the end of the demo session, the product owners who received a wow response will win 1 point and become eligible for the "wow demo of the week" award. There can only be one winner of the week, which is selected through a voting system. All attendees, participants, and observers cast their votes for the wow demo they deem to be the best of the week. There can only be one winner chosen through this democratic process. The wow demo winner of the week is rewarded with 3 points and a big celebratory round of applause.

We track the league's leaderboard weekly, and every six months, the team member with the most wow demo points is announced as the champion and celebrated with a grand ceremony, a trophy, and really meaningful prizes. The competition is set up to only celebrate the champion. We do not recognize runners-up with silver and bronze medals. This may sound aggressive, but it is highly effective at elevating the performance of the entire league through this intense, exciting, and fair competition.

Subsequently, a new season begins by extending an open invitation to new team members who have proven extreme ownership capabilities, and the poorest performing individuals from the prior season are dropped from the wow demo championship. The scoreboard is reset, and in the next six months, the league members compete on a weekly basis for the prestigious "wow demo" champion title.

The wow demo league has proven to do unbelievable wonders in boosting creativity, innovation, and productivity and, most importantly, inspiring an extreme sense of ownership in team members at all levels of the organization who would otherwise appear to be timid and average individual contributors.

BURN-ON TEAM RULE #9: Democratize ownership, and share the upside fairly.

Once you have broken down your big goals into achievable milestones based on the level of significance and priority, it is time to democratize ownership and share the upside fairly with your team. As a prerequisite to implementing such an incentive program, you need to vet the rightful owners from your most valuable team carefully. For example, any individual who does not win a single wow demo, ending the entire league season with 0 point, should not qualify as an owner. It is a strong indication that they aren't qualified enough for the job, or they don't care enough to make meaningful contributions to the company vision.

Such a shared ownership model should only be offered after ensuring that the individuals are highly capable and productive and have an owner mindset. You need to encourage them to truly invest themselves in their goals, the customers, and all other aspects of their project. They should be the ones most bothered about the success or failure of their mission.

It can be really empowering and freeing to have team members who care as much about your goals as you do. Together, you can go further and faster and build something greater than what would have been possible on your own. When you have multiple owners who can take the responsibility to successfully deliver their respective wow factors or deal breakers, the speed at which you move toward your end goal increases exponentially. This is how the magic of compounding can be leveraged to rapidly scale your business.

Once you have moved beyond the creative phase of figuring out what you'll build and how your MVT members will contribute to the mission, it's crucial to provide appropriate financial incentives to maintain the motivation of team members who embody the owner mindset. However, there needs to be a structured mechanism in place to hold individual team members accountable before setting up a fair and personalized upside incentive plan.

I have seen many companies expecting their employees to deliver above and beyond results by just offering them a base salary. Some offer a static bonus plan that is meant for status quo plus some minor incremental growth. This does not motivate 99.9 percent of people to go above and beyond their job requirements to contribute to the meaningful growth of the business. I believe that the sole purpose of the basic salary should be to cover the living expenses of the person. The upside incentive-based compensation should be what they really work for. It should motivate them to go above and beyond and contribute in an impactful way because they will also be rewarded in proportion to their contribution in achieving those meaningful outcomes that directly contribute to the success of the business.

The incentive plan should be structured such that it has an exponentially positive impact on their lives in proportion to their contribution toward the end result. For instance, if they earn $100,000 in annual base salary, the incentive should enable them to earn over a million dollars annually, provided that they bring at least a $15 million improvement in value to the business's top line.

Too many companies make the mistake of offering upside participation just based on the team member's tenure through stock incentive plans. I believe that this approach is extremely toxic and lazy. The tenure of employees by itself does not add value to your company. Instead, incentives and bonuses should be tied to the specific goals that align with each individual's responsibilities as an owner. These goals must be well articulated to avoid any ambiguity and should be highly aligned with the company's goals.

BURN-ON TEAM RULE #10: Use the SMARTS approach for setting goals.

Building anything great fast requires multiple owners who can take the responsibility to achieve their individual goals that will contribute to the grand scheme of things. To keep your team members motivated on this challenging journey, you need to have the right incentives in place so that it's a win-win for everyone. It cannot be done unless you have meticulously spelled out the outcomes that your MVT members must achieve. When you fail to define what success should mean for each team member by setting the right goal, it is hard to measure their progress and hold them accountable.

To ensure that everybody is clear on what they need to accomplish, you must follow the SMARTS approach for setting goals. SMARTS stands for Specific, Measurable, Achievable, Relevant, Time-Bound, and Stretch. Let's dive deeper into each of the SMARTS components to help you set the goals of your team members correctly.

Specific: While setting any goal for your MVT members, you should not leave any room for ambiguity. It is crucial to be specific on what they should aim to achieve. Goals that are vague or lack precision can leave your team without a clear sense of direction and focus. Getting granular in describing the target outcome will help in maximizing your team's productivity.

Measurable: You must always set quantifiable goals that can be easily measured using different key performance indicators. It allows you to monitor and measure the individual progress of each team member. In the dynamic startup ecosystem, where most businesses kick off their journey bootstrapped, there's a pressing need to ensure that every resource is utilized optimally.

Achievable: Setting goals that are not achievable can cause frustration among team members and also hamper their productivity. While striving for excellence is admirable, steering clear of the unattainable is important to keep your team members in the right frame of mind. You must take a pragmatic approach by assessing your objectives in the context of available resources, skill sets, and time constraints.

Relevant: Most businesses have limited resources in the early stages of their journey, so it's important to allocate them wisely to avoid failure. The goals for your team members should contribute effectively to your grandiose dream. You have to think of individual goals as different pieces of the same puzzle that are needed to complete the whole picture. You should always set goals that are relevant and aligned with your company's broader vision.

Time-Bound: You should consider your goals as specific points on a map, much like the milestones you want to reach in your entrepreneurial pursuit. Similar to a well-structured journey, assigning a time frame to your goals can prevent aimless wandering. It adds a sense of purpose and urgency, much like the ticking of a clock that drives your daily routine. When you add a timing element by setting a deadline for your goals, it pushes your team members to be more accountable and productive.

Stretch: Many a time, you have to push your team members a little beyond their set limits to achieve meaningful goals. You should aim to set goals that are challenging but achievable if you want your team members to evolve. Stretching the goals not only fosters growth and innovation but also enhances your team members' skills, making them more resilient and adaptable in the face of ever-evolving challenges.

By applying the SMARTS approach, you provide your team with a clear road map for achieving success. This method helps you avoid ambiguity, track progress effectively, and ensure that every goal contributes meaningfully to your project's advancement. Remember, setting goals isn't just about envisioning the strategic end result but also about creating a tactical plan to help you achieve it.

Time to Go Further and Faster

To go fast and far on the journey of building something meaningful that can wow the world, you must go together with the right people. It requires you to be focused and committed to creating your MVT by hiring individuals with the right foundational skills and a seeker mindset for the core roles in your organization.

Following the ten rules in this chapter will help you establish the strong foundational principles required to build and run a team that will burn on through the waves of ups and downs to achieve your end goal faster. By mastering these ten rules and embedding them into your organizational culture, you will become proficient at maximizing the potential of individuals and harnessing their collective abilities to achieve your shared company vision faster, further, and frequently.

CHAPTER 13 – KEY TAKEAWAYS

YOUR NOTES

_____

_____

_____

_____

_____

_____

_____

_____

_____

_____

_____

_____

CONCLUSION

Fads come and go every few months. Meaningful evolution happens every few years. However, game-changing disruption can only be experienced once or twice in one's lifetime.

As I articulate my parting words for you, the world is undergoing a game-changing transformation. We are just coming out of a very disruptive pandemic. In addition to leaving us with grim memories of human suffering and death, it has inadvertently triggered an unstoppable chain reaction far beyond the well-being and longevity of humans on this planet. Geopolitical and socioeconomic changes that were slowly brewing for years across the world have now exponentially accelerated.

Wait, there is more! To make matters even more volatile, we are now in the early stages of a new major zeitgeist. It is undisputed at this point that the latest mega innovation of AI will change our lives as profoundly as, if not more than, the last major zeitgeist that started three decades ago when computers and the Internet were introduced to the mainstream.

We are at an inflection point, and the only guarantee is that the future will be very different from the past as we know it. Such disruptions can be uncomfortable and brutal to the status quo when looking backward. However, on the brighter side, it can be a major opportunity when looking forward. The good news is that the state of the next era is not set in stone yet.

It is time for established and aspiring leaders to roll up their sleeves and go all in on the mission of building their ideas to lead us to a version of capitalism where businesses are generating more profits for their shareholders while delivering more value for their customers and doing more good for the communities that they serve.

Those who wait to see what happens will be surely disrupted. However, those who make their moves now and follow the principles of innovation done right will become the new disruptors. It is not going to be easy. Failing fast and failing often is the most likely outcome if you continue using the old mindset and toolsets that got us to this point. Now is the moment to accelerate your career and develop your legacy by building a better version of the world for the next generation with the ten secrets to succeed faster.

THE 10 SECRETS TO SUCCEED FASTER

#1 Dream Big and Do Bold

#2 Be a Seeker, Not a Bullshiter!

#3 Tap into the Zeitgeist!

#4 Turn Fear into your Superpower

#5 Work Smart before Working Hard

#6 What's your WOW Factor?

#7 Go Beyond with Your Wow Factor

#8 Choose the Right Day 1 Customer

#9 Pick the Right Battle at the Right Time

#10 Build a Burn-on Team

{ innovation done right }

Printed in the USA
CPSIA information can be obtained
at www.ICGtesting.com
JSHW011358110324
58993JS00012B/73/J